On orthodox Christianity:

"Nothing gives one a more spuriously good conscience than keeping rules, even if there has been a total absence of all real charity and faith."

On sorrow:

"It keeps on changing—like a winding road with quite a new landscape at each bend."

On happiness:

"The less one can think about happiness on earth, the less one suffers."

On dying:

"Though we struggle against things because we are afraid of them, it is often the other way round—we get afraid *because* we struggle."

> "Pick up [this] little book and sift through for . . . an appreciation of that inimitable being that was C. S. Lewis." —*Ave Maria*

C. S. LEWIS (1898-1963) was a fellow and tutor of English at Oxford from 1925 to 1954. He was noted equally for his literary scholarship and for his intellectual and witty writings. Among his most important works are *An Allegory of Love* and *The Screwtape Letters*, the latter—a humorously ironic treatment of the theme of salvation—bringing him a wide and popular audience. He is also the author of *Out of the Silent Planet, Perelandra* and *That Hideous Strength*, an outer-space trilogy with deeply moral overtones. He wrote children's books—perhaps the best known *The Lion, the Witch and the Wardrobe*—and the autobiographical *Surprised by Joy*. He died during his tenure as a professor of Medieval and Renaissance English at Cambridge in 1963.

LETTERS TO AN
AMERICAN LADY

C. S. Lewis

Edited by CLYDE S. KILBY

William B. Eerdmans Publishing Company
Grand Rapids, Michigan

LETTERS TO AN AMERICAN LADY

Published by Pyramid Publications for Wm. B. Eerdmans Publishing Co.

This edition published September, 1971

Reprinted, July 1987

Copyright © 1967 by Wm. B. Eerdmans Publishing Co.
All Rights Reserved

Library of Congress Catalog Card Number: 67-30853

Printed in the United States of America

WILLIAM B. EERDMANS PUBLISHING CO.
255 Jefferson, S.E., Grand Rapids, Michigan 49502, U.S.A.

Preface

When C. S. Lewis wrote the first letter in the following collection he was 51 years old and long established at Magdalen College, Oxford, as university lecturer and tutor. He had published twenty books, of which four, the outcome of his scholarly pursuits, had given him a wide reputation as medievalist and literary critic. Most of the other sixteen were the results of Lewis's conversion, at 29, to Christianity and were divided between expository and creative works. Among the former were *The Problem of Pain* and *Miracles* and among the latter *The Screwtape Letters*, a space trilogy called *Out of the Silent Planet*, *Perelandra*, and *That Hideous Strength*. In that year was published *The Lion, the Witch and the Wardrobe*, the first of a series of seven children's books with clear Christian overtones.

Almost twenty years earlier he and his brother Warren, both bachelors, had settled in a house called The Kilns, four miles east of Oxford and abutting a hillside of fine trees rising above tangled vines and blackberry bushes and, at its base, a small quarry lake where they could swim in water apparently once used by the poet Shelley to sail his little paper boats. With them lived Mrs. Moore, a widowed mother of one of Lewis's friends who was a casualty on the French front in World War I. Despite the fact that Mrs. Moore during her last years succeeded in making life at The Kilns something of a continuous misery, Lewis treated her with filial love as long as she lived.

Long since Lewis had completed brilliantly his study at University College, Oxford, and had been elected to Magdalen. He had sometimes found his tutorials boring, especially when his student could not rise to the high intellectual bait that was offered, but his lectures, both from their content and expression, were often crowded to the point of standing room only. One of his students said that he had "more knowledge at his finger tips" than anyone he had ever known, and another described his mind as "the most exact and penetrating" he had encountered.

The letters in this volume pretty well identify the events in Lewis's life after 1950. He traveled little and in general lived the sort of life he preferred—scholarship, lectures, daily walks whenever possible and long cross-country hikes with friends at seasonable periods, conversation (especially that engendered in the Inklings, a group of intellectuals who met on Thursday evenings), and reading and writing. Three of the main events of his later life were his marriage to Joy Davidman in 1957, her death a little over three years later, and his election to the chair of Medieval and Renaissance English at Cambridge. Lewis died on November 22, 1963, a week before his sixty-fifth birthday and the same afternoon on which President John F. Kennedy was assassinated.

These letters accentuate rather than change the character of Lewis as it is generally known. In them are his antipathy to journalism, advertising, snobbery, psychoanalysis, to the false and the patent, to wheels and stir and "administration" and the multitude of petty or insidious practices that sap personal and national freedom. And we must not fail to add his antipathy to letter-writing. In his autobiography he says that one essential of the happy life is "that a man would have almost no mail and never dread the postman's knock." Yet here we have enough letters to fill a book written to one person in a far country whom he never expected to meet in this world. Although this is one of the longest of Lewis's correspondences, it is not the only one running to a hundred or more letters.

Here is a man who could have found a whole bag of reasons to justify pitching his mail into the wastepaper basket. He was often worked to the point of distraction by his university duties, a man whose successful books both in scholarship and religion clamor for more of the same sort, a man with a remarkable combination of logic and imagination that might produce such books almost endlessly, a man who by nature tends to avoid strangers and loves the inner world of ideas and the intimate circle of old friends. Yet this man meticulously endeavors to answer, sometimes with an arm so rheumatic that he can hardly push the pen, the vast correspondence falling into his hands from around the world. Why?

The main cause was that Lewis believed taking time out to advise or encourage another Christian was both a humbling of one's talents before the Lord and also as much the work of the Holy Spirit as producing a book. John Wesley somewhere in his journal during the days when vast crowds were hearing him says that on a given night he preached to only one poor sinner at the inn. Lewis had the same dedicated attitude, the belief that one's days and his talents are given him not for private expenditure but to be used in all lowliness within the will of God. Though the flesh abhorred it, he mortified the flesh. There seems no shred of idea that these letters might eventually be published and thus take their place beside his other

7

Christian works. They come to the point immediately, cover it and conclude. They are not "literary" letters. There is little description, little reminiscence, little urbanity, wit, sentiment, little even that is reflective. There is little of Lewis's lifelong interest in fantasy, joy, *Sehnsucht*. His academic and scholarly interests get brief mention only.

The obvious thrust of these letters is spiritual encouragement and guidance and it is chiefly here that they have their value. There is the hope that his soul may stay utterly responsive to God and his behavior never lapse into mere rule-keeping. Like the Fathers, there is the conviction that holiness is actually to be practiced by the Christian and the belief that if only ten percent of the world's population had holiness the rest of the people would be converted quickly. When his correspondent hesitates to accept financial aid, he reminds her that all men are charity cases and that God "foots all our bills." Concerning God's goodness, he points out that shadows make up half the beauty of the world and that it is not necessarily different with the shadows coming into our lives if we recognize them as permitted by perfect Goodness. As in all his other writings, Lewis hews the sharpest of lines between the utter and continuous practice of Christianity and our feelings. We are to *do* and let our feelings be as they may. Also as elsewhere, Lewis emphasizes that God's grace is sufficient for this day, this hour, not for all the troubles we can imagine for the future or remember from the past. And here, as always, we find Lewis's firm belief in the resurrection of the body and the felicities of heaven. "It'll be fun when we meet at last," he tells her. They are indeed Christian letters.

But they are not without glimpses of Lewis the man, lover of cats and dogs, of the first cuckoo and the first crocus of spring, of Lewis getting up to prepare his own breakfast and do his chores during the much-loved "empty, silent, dewy, cobwebby hours" of the morning. There is Lewis announcing that he may soon be both a husband and a widower, then finding that something like a miracle has taken place and Joy's cancer has seemingly disappeared, and then, later, the fierce shock of her death. Because both Lewis and his correspondent had in common a mélange of physical troubles, we learn more here than anywhere else of his increasingly numerous maladies that were finally to join hands in his decease. There is Lewis the dreader of poverty who, it became known after his death, gave away two-thirds of his income and even then was not satisfied with the extent of his charities.

At her own request, the identity of Lewis's correspondent is withheld. A widow four years older than Lewis, she was described by one friend as "very charming, gracious, a southern aristocratic lady who loves to talk and speaks well." Once financially independent, she had fallen upon privation and, what was worse, serious family problems. In due course Lewis arranged through his American publishers a small stipend for her, and this continues to the present. About the time the correspondence began she turned from the Episcopal Church to the Roman Catholic. Twice she has been so near death that the last rites of the church were administered. Though I have occasionally felt the necessity of a footnote, I believe her interests (except the family problems, which are excised) explain themselves. She is a writer of reviews articles, poems and stories.

The aim in editing has been as far as possible to leave the letters just as Lewis wrote them. I have

9

expanded some of his unusual abbreviations, such as *v.* for *very, wh.* for *which,* etc. His interesting multiformity in the writing of dates is retained, including of course the British method of, for instance, "26/10/50" for October 26, 1950. Included among the letters are a few by his wife Joy Lewis, his brother W. H. Lewis and his personal secretary Walter Hooper. The reason for inclusion in each instance is explained within the letter itself.

As agent of Wheaton College, I should like to express our sincerest gratitude to the recipient of these letters both for donating them to our library and also for graciously offering us the privilege of publication. We are also grateful to the Executors of Lewis's estate for their kind cooperation. The Reverend Walter Hooper, Chaplain of Wadham College, Oxford, has shown his usual willingness to render every help possible, including an examination of the manuscript and suggestions for improvement. Mrs. Ruth Cording and my wife Martha have been most useful in transcribing the letters and in other ways. Mr. Robert Golter, Librarian of Wheaton College, has worked closely with me in various ways. To Major W. H. Lewis for his friendship and encouragement I feel endless gratitude.

Wheaton College   —CLYDE S. KILBY

Magdalen College
Oxford
26/10/50

Dear Mrs.————

Thank you for your most kind and encouraging letter. I should need to be either of angelic humility or diabolical pride not to be pleased at all the things you say about my books. (I think, by the way, you have all the ones that would matter to you). May I assure you of my deep sympathy in all the very grievous troubles that you have had. May God continue to support you; that He has done so till now, is apparent from the fact that you are not warped or embittered. I will have you in my prayers. With all good wishes.

Yours sincerely
C. S. Lewis

Magdalen College
Oxford
Nov. 10th 1952

Dear Mrs. ————

It is a little difficult to explain how I feel that tho' you have taken a way which is not for me[1] I nevertheless can congratulate you—I suppose because your faith and joy are so obviously increased. Naturally, I do not draw from that the same conclusions as you— but there is no need for us to start a controversial correspondence! I believe we are very near to one another, but not because I am at all on the Romeward frontier of my own communion. I believe that, in the present divided state of Christendom, those who are at the heart of each division are all closer to one another than those who are at the fringes. I would even carry this beyond the borders of Chris-

[1] She had left the Episcopal Church to become a Roman Catholic.

tianity: how much more one has in common with a *real* Jew or Muslim than with a wretched liberalising, occidentalised specimen of the same categories. Let us by all means pray for one another: it is perhaps the only form of "work for re-union" which never does anything but good. God bless you.

Yours most sincerely
C. S. Lewis

Magdalen College,
Oxford
Jan. 19th 1953

Dear Mrs. ————

Thank you for your kind letter of Dec. 29th which arrived to-day. I am afraid I have no idea what the first editions of *Screwtape* or the *Divorce* sell at: I haven't even got a first of the former myself. But you would be foolish to spend a cent more on them than the published prices: both belong to the worst war-period and are scrubby little things on rotten paper—your American editions are far nicer. Your letter was most cheering and I am full of agreements. Of course we'll help each other in our prayers. God bless you.

Yours most sincerely
C. S. Lewis

Magdalen College
Oxford, England
4/iii/53

Dear Mrs. ————

Thank you for your letter of Feb. 26 which arrived today. ... *Eldila* is the true plural: but you can Anglicise it as *eldils!*[1]

---

[1] Eldils are beings in Lewis's *Out of the Silent Planet*, *Perelandra* and *That Hideous Strength*.

I am delighted that your lecturer approved my angels. I was very definitely trying to smash the 19th century *female* angel. I believe *no* angel ever appears in Scripture without exciting terror: they always have to begin by saying "Fear not". On the other hand the Risen Lord excites terror only when mistaken for a ghost, i.e. when not recognised as *risen*. For we are in one most blessed sense *nearer* to Him than to them: partly of course because He has deigned to share our humanity, but partly, I take it, because every creature is nearer to its creator than it can be to superior *creatures*. By the way, none of my Eldila would be anything like so high up the scale as Cherubim and Seraphim. Those orders are engaged wholly in contemplation, not with ruling the lower creatures. Even the Annunciation was done by—if I may so put it!—a "mere archangel". Did your lecturer point out my heavy debt to Ezekiel?

Of course I knew you weren't asking for a copy of a "First": but I wanted to explain why I was not offering one—quite a different matter!

I also am having a kind of flu' that seems never to get beyond early convalescence, tho' nothing like so acute as yours. For that, and all else, deepest sympathy. Let us continue to pray for each other.

Yours most sincerely
C. S. Lewis

Magdalen College
Oxford, England
31/3/53

Dear Mrs. ———

I've no time for a proper letter to-day but this is just a scrape of the pen to thank you for yours of the 27th and to wish you a very blessed Easter. . . .

Apropos of horrid little fat baby "cherubs", did I

mention that Heb. *Kherub* is from the same root as *Gryphon?* That shows what they're really like!

Yours
C. S. Lewis

Magdelan College
Oxford, England
17/4/53

Dear Mrs. ————

I'm not quite so shocked as you by the story of Charles and Mary. If even adult and educated Christians in trying to think of the Blessed Trinity have to guard constantly against falling into the heresy of Tritheism, what can we expect of children. And "another of whom he was not quite sure" is perhaps no bad *beginning* for a knowledge about the Holy Ghost.

About my fairy-tales, there are three published by Macmillan, New York (*The Lion, the Witch and the Wardrobe, Prince Caspian,* and *The Voyage of the Dawn Treader*). Local bookshops are often very unhelpful. If your friend wants these books she should, of course, write to the publisher at New York.

I expect there *is* a photo of me somewhere, but my brother, who knows where things are, is away and I couldn't find it to-day. Ask me again at a more favourable hour!—if you still have the fancy for this very undecorative object.

I'd sooner pray for God's mercy than for His justice on my friends, my enemies, and myself.

With all good wishes.

Yours sincerely
C. S. Lewis

Dear Mrs. ———

There's very little time today, so I must be short. I am afraid it is certainly true in England that Christians are in the minority. But remember, the change from, say, thirty years ago, consists largely in the fact that *nominal* Christianity has died out, so that only those who really believe now profess. The old conventional church-going of semi-believers or almost total unbelievers is a thing of the past. Whether the real thing is rarer than it was would be hard to say. Fewer children are brought up to it: but adult conversions are very frequent. . . .

I enclose a copy of the only photo which I have at the moment; it's only a passport one I'm afraid.

Yours most sincerely,
C. S. Lewis

Magdalen College,
Oxford
May 30th, 1953

Dear Mrs. ———

Thank you for your letter of the 26th. . . .

Yes, we are always told that the present widespread apostasy must be the fault of the clergy, not of the laity. If I were a parson I should always try to dwell on the faults of the clergy: being a layman, I think it more wholesome to concentrate on those of the laity. I am rather sick of the modern assumption that, for all events, "WE", the people, are never responsible: it is always our rulers, or ancestors, or parents, or education, or anybody but precious "US". WE are apparently perfect and blameless. Don't you believe it. Nor do I think the Church of England holds out many attractions to the worldly. There is more real poverty, even actual want, in English vicarages than there is in the homes of casual labourers.

I look forward to Martin's "appreciations". Yes, we have the word "dither"—and the thing too. And our offices are in a dither too. This is so common that I suspect there must be something in the very structure of a modern office which creates Dither. Otherwise why does our "College Office" find full time work for a crowd of people in doing what the President of the College, 100 years ago, did in his spare time without a secretary and without a typewriter? (The more noise, heat, and smell a machine produces the more power is being wasted!) I'd rather like to see one of your hail storms: our climate is in comparison, very tame. Have you read S. V. Benet's *Western Star?* Excellent, I think.

Yours sincerely
C. S. Lewis

Magdalen College.
Oxford.
June 16th, 1953

Dear Mrs.

It was a kind thought on your part to send on these two little items. Whether it's good for me to hear them is another matter! One of the things that make it easier to believe in Providence is the fact that in all trains, hotels, restaurants and other public places I have only *once* seen a stranger reading a book of mine, tho' my friends encounter this phenomenon fairly often. Things are really very well arranged. I hope you keep well? With all blessings.

Yours
C. S. Lewis

Dear Mrs. ————

Thank you for your letter of the 18th. I am very sorry to hear of your fall (that sounds sinister, doesn't it!) They are very nasty things: even worse than the subsequent pain, I think, is the dreadful split second in which one knows one is falling and it's too late to do anything about it. It always brings back to one vividly one's childish days when a fall was one of the commonest catastrophes, and I think it really hurt then more than it does now: one of the many things that people forget when they wish they were children again! You and I who still enjoy fairy tales have less reason to wish actual childhood back. We have kept its pleasures and added some grown-up ones as well. One hasn't kept the *senses*, though. What a comparatively tasteless thing an egg or a strawberry is now! Yes: I think the palate is the only part of me that need regret the early years. . . . By the way did the reviewers *mean* "writes like a woman" to be dispraise? Are the poems of Sappho or, if it comes to that, the *Magnificat*, to be belittled on the same ground?

You are quite right, I didn't go to the Coronation. I approve of all that sort of thing immensely and I was deeply moved by all I heard of it; but I'm not a man for crowds and Best Clothes. The weather was frightful.

As you had forgotten what called for my remarks about WE, THE PEOPLE, so I have now quite forgotten what the said remarks were! That is one way correspondence differs from conversation. On the other hand neither party can interrupt! Oh—I'm often in a *dither*: usually when I've made two engagements for the same time in different places.

Yours
C. S. Lewis

Magdalen College
Oxford
July 10, 1953

Dear Mrs. ————

Thanks for your letter of June 30th. I found the poem interesting—especially *metrically* interesting. From that point of view L. 3 is the important one: notice how it keeps the five beats because one is forced to give full value to the two long monosyllables—"one goal"—Remémber the ónly, the óne góal of life". L. 2 where you collapse into a 4 beat-rhythm is not, I think, nearly so good. "God speed" at the end is a trifle weak isn't it? And if one puts it into God's mouth—as the context invites one to do—a little comic: like in the old miracle play where God, in a moment of excitement, is made to exclaim "By God!"

You know, over here people did *not* get that fairy-tale feeling about the coronation. What impressed most who saw it was the fact that the Queen herself appeared to be quite overwhelmed by the sacramental side of it. Hence, in the spectators, a feeling of (one hardly knows how to describe it)—awe —pity—pathos—mystery. The pressing of that huge, heavy crown on that small, young head becomes a sort of symbol of the situation of *humanity* itself: humanity called by God to be His vice-gerent and high priest on earth, yet feeling so inadequate. As if He said "In my inexorable love I shall lay upon the dust that you are glories and dangers and responsibilities beyond your understanding". Do you see what I mean? One has missed the whole point unless one feels that we have all been crowned and that coronation is somehow, if splendid, a tragic splendour. . . .

By the way isn't a motor-car the *safest* place to be in a thunderstorm: isolated from the earth by rubber tyres which are non-conductors? Or do I only display my ignorance?

Yours
C. S. Lewis

Magdalen etc.
Aug 1st [1953]

Dear Mrs. ————

Thanks for yours of the 16th. Our climatic troubles are just the opposite of yours; one of the coldest and wettest summers I remember. But I'd dislike your heat very much more than our cold. I am so glad you gave me an account of the lovely priest. How little people know who think that holiness is dull. When one meets the real thing (and perhaps, like you, I have met it only once) it is irresistible. If even 10% of the world's population had it, would not the whole world be converted and happy before a year's end? Yes, I too think there is lots to be said for being no longer young; and I do most heartily agree that it is just as well to be past the age when one expects or desires to attract the other sex. It's natural enough in our species, as in others, that the young birds should show off their plumage—in the mating season. But the trouble in the modern world is that there's a tendency to rush all the birds on to that age as soon as possible and then keep them there as late as possible, thus losing all the real value of the *other* parts of life in a senseless, pitiful attempt to prolong what, after all, is neither its wisest, its happiest, or most innocent period. I suspect merely commercial motives are behind it all: for it is at the showing-off age that birds of both sexes have least sales-resistance! Naturally I can have no views on a choice between your home town and Washington any more than on one between Omsk and Teheran! but of course you shall have my prayers. Sorry to hear about the fall: they're nasty things. I must stop now, for I'm dead tired from standing at catalogue-shelves in a library all morning verifying titles of books and editions. I think, like the Irishman in the story "I'd sooner *walk* 10 miles than *stand* one". I go to Ireland on the 11th so don't be surprised if you don't hear from me again till the end of September. All blessings.

Yours
C. S. Lewis

Magdalen
Aug 10th 53

Dear Mrs. ————

I have just got your letter of the 6th. Oh I *do* so sympathise with you: job-hunting, even in youth, is a heartbreaking affair and to have to go back to it now must be simply—I was going to say "simply Hell", but no one who is engaged in prayer and humility, as you are, can be there, so I'd better say "Purgatory". (We have as a matter of fact good authorities for calling it something better than Purgatory. We are told that even those tribulations which fall upon us by necessity, if embraced for Christ's sake, become as meritorious as *voluntary* sufferings and every missed meal can be converted into a fast if taken in the right way.) I suppose—tho' the person who is *not* suffering feels shy about saying it to the person who *is*—that it is good for us to be cured of the illusion of "independence". For of course independence, the state of being indebted to no one, is eternally impossible.

Who, after all, is more totally dependent than what we call the man "of independent means". Every shirt he wears is made by other people out of other organisms and the only difference between him and us is that even the money whereby he pays for it was earned by other people. Of course you *ought* to be dependent on your daughter and son-in-law. Support of parents is a most ancient and universally acknowledged duty. And if you come to find yourself dependent on anyone else you mustn't mind. But I am very, very sorry. I'm a panic-y person about money myself (which is a most shameful confession and a thing dead against Our Lord's words) and poverty frightens me more than anything else except large spiders and the tops of cliffs: one is sometimes even tempted to say that if God wanted us to live like the lilies of the field He might have given us an organism more like theirs! But of course He is right. And when you meet anyone who *does* live like the lilies, one *sees* that He is. God keep you and encourage you. I am just about to go off to Ireland where I shall be moving about, so I shan't hear from you for several weeks. All blessings and deepest sympathy.

Yours
C. S. Lewis

Magdalen College
Oxford
Nov. 6/53

Dear Mrs. ————

Oh I *am* glad, I *am* glad. And here's a thing worth recording. Of course I have been praying for you daily, as always, but latterly have found myself doing so with much more concern and especially about 2 nights ago, with such a strong feeling how very nice it would be, if God willed, to get a letter from you with good news. And then, as if by magic (indeed it is the whitest magic in the world) the letter comes to-day. Not (lest I should indulge in folly) that your relief had not in fact occurred *before* my prayer, but as if, in tenderness for my puny faith God moved me to pray with especial earnestness just before He was going to give me the thing. How true that our prayers are really His prayers; He speaks to Himself through us. I am also most moved at hearing how you were supported thro' the period of anxiety. For one *is* sometimes tempted to think that if He wanted us to be as un-anxious as the lilies of the field He really might have given us a constitution more like theirs! But then when the need comes *He* carries out in us His otherwise impossible instructions. In fact He always has to do all the things—all the prayers, all the virtues. No new doctrine, but newly come home to me. Forgive a short letter, quite inadequate to the subject: I am at present just so busy (tho' not unhappily so) that I don't know if I'm on my head or my heels. God bless you.

Yours
C. S. Lewis

Magdalen College
Oxford
27/xi/53

Dear Mrs. ————

Thank you for your letter of Nov. 23rd. We have a good many things in common at the moment, for I also am dead tired (cab-horse tired) and I also have sinusitis. I don't think we exactly "call it catarrh" over here. Intense catarrh is *one* symptom of sinusitis, and as none of us have heard of s. till quite lately I suppose cases of it used to be wrongly diagnosed as mere catarrh. I find myself that when it produces most catarrh it produces least pain and vice versa. About sleep: do you find that the great secret (if one can do it) is not to *care* whether you sleep? Sleep is a jade who scorns her suitors but woos her scorners. I feel exactly as you do about the horrid commercial racket they have made out of Christmas. I send no cards and give no presents except to children.

It is fun to see you agreeing with what you believe to be *my* views on prayer: well you may, for they are not mine but scriptural. "Our prayers are God talking to Himself" is only Romans, VIII, 26-27. And "praying to the end" is of course our old acquaintance, the parable of the Unjust Judge.

I am sure you will be glad to hear that your recent adventures have been a great support and "corroboration" to me. I am also very conscious (and was especially so while praying for you during your workless time) that anxiety is not only a pain which we must ask God to assuage but also a weakness we must ask Him to pardon—for He's told us take no care for the morrow. The news that you had been almost miraculously guarded from that sin and spared that pain and hence the good hope that we shall all find the like mercy when our bad times come, has strengthened me much. God bless you.

Yours
C. S. Lewis

Magdalen College
Oxford
Jan. 1st 1954

Dear Mrs. ————

Thanks for your letter of the 28th, to which I'm afraid I can manage only a very small answer, for Christmas mails have "got me down". This season is to me mainly hard, gruelling work—write, write, write, till I wickedly say that if there were less *good will* (going through the post) there would be more *peace on earth.* By Jove, I do sympathise with you about the sinus (I am warned by everyone who has ever had it *not* at any price to have the operation. One doctor said that he would like to prosecute any surgeon who did it. This concerns you too!). I am sure that when God allows some cause like illness or a 'bus-strike or a broken alarm clock to keep us from Mass, He has His own good reasons for not wishing us to go to it on that occasion. He who took care lest the 5000 should "faint" going home on an empty stomach may be trusted to know when we need *bed* even more than Mass. I don't think there is anything superstitious in your story about the Voice. These visions or "auditions" at the moment of death are all very well attested: quite in a different category from ordinary ghost stories. I am so glad people liked your poem, which deserved it, and that you liked mine[1] of which (a very unusual thing for me) I can't now remember a single word. But I *must* stop; wishing and praying for you "a happy issue out of all your afflictions" and better days in 1954.

Yours
C. S. Lewis

Magdalen College
Oxford
24/1/54

Dear Mrs. ———

Thanks for the lovely bundle of letters and pictures from the ——— family which, as you anticipated, I revelled in: I have written them a joint letter—not mentioning the poem as I gather you are not supposed to have a copy. They sound a delightful family.

[1] See "The Nativity" in Lewis's *Poems.*

But surely you are not going to put the whole trilogy in their hands? I should have thought *That Hideous Strength* both unsuitable and unintelligible to children, and even *Perelandra* rather doubtful. I hope you have got rid of that cold. There seems no way of guarding against them, does there? One part of me almost envies you that deep snow: *real* snow. This is very late at night and my writing is dreadful, so I must stop. All blessings.

Yours
C. S. Lewis

Magdalen College,
Oxford
26/1/54

Dear Mrs. ————

Thanks for yours of the 23rd and for copy of my verses, which I had almost totally forgotten. 'Pon my word, they're not so bad as I feared. I'm very sorry about your cold. We mustn't let these modern doctors get us down by calling a cold a *virus* and a sore throat a *streptococcus*, you know! (Do you ever read Montaigne? He says "The peasants make everything easier by the names they use. To them a consumption is only a cough and a cancer only a stomachache"). You should have stayed tucked up in a warm bed all that day instead of trying to write and walking up and down the room.

We wouldn't call Alfred and Egbert and all those the "British" line. They are the "English" line, the Angles, who come from Angel in South Denmark. By the *British* line we'd mean the Celtic line that goes back through the Tudors to Cadwallader and thence to Arthur, Uther, Cassibelan, Lear, Lud, Brut, Aeneas, Jupiter. The present royal family can claim descent from both the British and the English lines. So, I suppose, can most of us: for since one has 2 parents, 4 grandparents, 16 great-grandparents, and so on, one is presumably descended from nearly everyone who was alive in this island in the year 600 A.D. In the long run one is related to everyone on the planet: in that quite literal sense we are all "one flesh". Of course I don't mean to ignore (in fact I find it nice) the distinction between a peasant's grandson like myself and those of noble blood. I only observe that the nobility lies not in the ancient descent (which is common to us all) but in having been for so many generations illustrious that more of the steps are *recorded*. I do hope you'll be better by the time this reaches you.

Yours
€. S. Lewis

Magdalen College
Oxford
Feb 22/54

Dear Mrs.

I am very sorry indeed to hear that anxieties again assail you. (By the way, don't "weep inwardly" and get a sore throat. If you must weep, weep: a good honest howl! I suspect we—and especially, my sex—don't cry enough now-a-days. Aeneas and Hector and Beowulf, Roland and Lancelot blubbered like schoolgirls, so why shouldn't we?) You were wonderfully supported in your worries last time; I shall indeed pray that it may be so again.

I didn't object to the family reading the trilogy[1] on the ground that it would be too difficult—that would do no harm—but because in the last one there is so

---

[1] *Out of the Silent Planet, Perelandra* and *That Hideous Strength.*

much evil, in a form not, I think, suitable for their age, and many specifically sexual problems which it would do them no good to think of at present. I daresay the *Silent Planet* is alright: *Perelandra*, little less so: T.H.S. most unsuitable.

I don't think an *appreciation* of ancient and noble blood is "snobbery" at all. What is snobbery is a greedy desire to know those who have it, or a mean desire to flatter them, or a conceited desire to boast of their acquaintance. I think it quite legitimate to feel that such things give an added interest to a person who is nice on other grounds, just as a hotel which was nice on other grounds would have an added charm for me if it was also a building with "historic interest".

I write in great haste—I can't, like you, do it in working hours! But you're nothing to Lamb: as far as I can make out all his letters, which now fill two volumes, were written in the office. Happy days those.

Well, I hope I shall have better news in your next. God bless you.

Yours
C. S. Lewis

Magdalen College
Oxford
March 10/54

Dear Mrs. ————

I am sorry things are not better. I am very puzzled by people like your Committee Secretary, people who are just nasty. I find it easier to understand the great crimes, for the raw material of them exists in us all; the mere disagreeableness which seems to spring from no recognisable passion is mysterious. (Like the total stranger in a train of whom I once asked "Do you know when we get to Liverpool" and who replied "I'm not paid to answer your questions: ask the guard"). I have found it more among Boys than anyone else. That makes me think it really comes from inner insecurity—a dim sense that one is Nobody, a strong determination to be Somebody, and a belief that this can be achieved by arrogance. Probably *you*, who can't hit back, come in for a good deal of *resentful* arrogance aroused by others on whom she doesn't vent it, because they *can*. (A bully in an Elizabethan play, having been sat on by a man he dare not fight, says "I'll go home and beat all my servants"). But I mustn't encourage you to go on thinking about her: that, after all, is almost the greatest evil nasty people can do us—to become an obsession, to haunt our minds. A brief prayer for them, and then away to other subjects, is the thing, if one can only stick to it. I hope the other job will materialise.

I thought the poem by that woman was very good Christianity, but not a very good poem: no rhythmic vitality, no reason why the lines should end where they do, and no vocalic melody. But then I'm old fashioned. I think *vers libre* succeeds only in a few exceptional poems and its prevalence has really ruined the art.

I too had mumps after I was grown up. I didn't mind it as long as I had the temperature: but when one came to convalescence and a convalescent appetite and even *thinking* of food started the salivation and the pain—ugh! I never realised "the disobedience in our members" so clearly before. Verily "He that but looketh on a plate of ham and eggs to lust after it, hath already committed breakfast with it in his heart" (or in his glands).

I shall wait anxiously for all your news, always

praying not only for a happy issue but that you may be supported in all interim anxieties.

Yours
C. S. Lewis

Magdalen College
Oxford
March 31st 54

Dear Mary

(I return the compliment by telling you that my friends all call me Jack). I am sorry the persecution still goes on. I had that sort of thing at school, and in the army, and here too when I was a junior fellow, and it does very much darken life. I suppose (tho' it seems a hard saying) we should mind humiliation less if [we] were humbler. It is, at any rate, a form of suffering which we can try to offer, in our small way, along with the supreme humiliation of Christ Himself. There is, if you notice it, a very great deal in the N.T. about His humiliations as distinct from His sufferings in general. And it is the humble and meek who have all the blessings in the *Magnificat*. So your position is, spiritually, far safer than the opposite one. But don't think I don't know how much easier it is to preach than practice. Yes, I have read Martin's story, with much interest. I don't think the nonchalance of the policeman was one of its merits, though: I think it only means that Martin (very naturally) is still at the stage of imagining an event but not yet at the stage of imagining the reactions. Of course this has a whimsically comic effect for a grown-up reader, but that is accidental. How right you are to see that anger (even when directed against oneself) "worketh not the righteousness of God". One must never be *either* content with, *or* impatient with, oneself. My old confessor (now dead) used to impress on me the need for the 3 Patiences: patience with God, with my neighbour, with oneself. Need one ever be anxious about mumps in a woman? It sometimes is serious in men if they get it as adults. Yes, I'm sick of our Abracadabrist poets. What gives the show away is that their professed admirers give quite contradictory interpretations of the same poem—I'm prepared to believe that an unintelligible picture is really a very good horse if all its admirers tell me so; but when one says it's a horse, and the next that it's a ship, and the third that it's an orange, and the fourth that it's Mt. Everest, I give it up. All blessings.

Yours
Jack

P.S.—You speak of the "cult of the OBSTUSE". Do you mean ABSTRUSE, OBTUSE or OBSCURE? Lord Dunsany is a glorious writer in prose: try *The Charwoman's Shadow*.

Magdalen College,
Oxford.
17th April 1954.

Dear Mary

Only a scrap, for everyone writes to me at Easter, so that what ought to be a bright spot in the year threatens to become for me a very dark one. Will you, please, always avoid "holiday" periods in writing to me?

All blessings, and I hope the new job will go nicely.

Yours,
Jack

Magdalen College
Oxford
May 27th 1954

Dear Mary

Thanks for yours of the 24th. I am glad to hear you have moved into pleasanter quarters and hope there will be a great blessing both upon them and on the new job. The saving of time and money on bus travel is a great point: or rather, if your experience is at all like mine, the time spent not in travelling but in waiting at 'bus stops, often in very cold or very hot weather. I've no idea what a "pent-house apartment" may be! I'm sorry to disappoint you with such a scrap of a letter, but the rush is still on (I foresee no end to it before August) and the mails have been above the average for weeks now: I don't know why. It's a cold backward spring here but there are some lovely days. Sunshine just flirts with us and then disappears. You are always in my prayers.

Yours ever
Jack

Magdalen College
Oxford.
14th. June 1954.

Dear Mary

Yes, I'm through the Easter letters, and now examining. I have averaged 20 scripts a day (including Sundays) for six weeks—the viva voce examinations will take eight hours a day. I shall become human again at about the end of September. Meanwhile, love and good wishes.

Yours,
Jack

Dear Mary

I got back from my holiday yesterday, to the usual
pile of letters which makes one wonder if holidays are
worth it. (I had been in Ireland, Donegal, which is
lovely. All the mountains look like mountains in a
story, and there are wooded valleys, and golden
sands, and the smell of peat from every cottage). I'm
glad I wasn't in your heatwave! Your description fully
reconciles me to the unusually cold and wet summer
we have had here. But I *would* like to have a stage-
door acquaintance with a star Rabbit! I was very glad
to hear about——. (How different girls are from
boys. To me at her age clothes would have been the
dullest of all presents). About the lack of religious
education: of course you must be grieved, but remember how much religious education has exactly the opposite effect to that which was intended, how many
hard atheists come from pious homes. May we not
hope, with God's mercy, that a similarly opposite effect may be produced in her case? Parents are not
Providence: their bad intentions may be frustrated
as their good ones. Perhaps prayers as a secret indulgence which Father disapproves may have a charm
they lacked in houses where they were commanded.
And congratulations on [being included in] the Vir-
ginia Anthology. . . . I can well understand your fears
about old age. And of course you are doing the very
best thing in meditating on the sufferings of Our
Lord. (Drat—on top of all the letters comes a telephone call to say that "a lady" in the Lodge wants to
come across to see me). I've been made a Professor
at Cambridge, which will mean less work and there-
fore of course ('tis the way of the world) more pay.

I've also got rheumatism, but not very bad: only like always feeling you've just had a 20 mile walk on a rather hard road! It is nice to be able to write again; I've had a very hectic summer. You are always in my prayers.

> Yours
> Jack

> Magdalen College,
> Oxford.
> Oct 9th 54

Dear Mary

Thanks for your letter of the 6th, enclosing poem which I enjoyed. Fairies—the people of the *Shidhe* (pronounced Shee)—are still believed in many parts of Ireland and greatly feared. I stayed at a lovely bungalow in Co. Louth where the wood was said to be haunted by a ghost *and* by fairies. But it was the latter who kept the country people away. Which gives you the point of view—a ghost much *less* alarming than a fairy. A Donegal man told a parson I know that one night when he was walking home on the beach a woman came up out of the sea and "her face was as pale as gold". I have seen a leprechaun's shoe, given to a doctor by a grateful patient. It was the length, and hardly more than the breadth, of my forefinger, made of soft leather and slightly worn on the sole. But get out of your head any ideas of comic or delightful creatures. They are greatly dreaded, and called "the good people" not because they *are* good but in order to propitiate them. I have found no trace of anyone believing or ever having believed (in England or Ireland) in the *tiny* fairies of Shakespeare, which are a purely literary invention. Leprechauns are smaller than men, but most fairies are of human size, some larger. I don't know that a professorial chair or anything else will now provide for a comfortable old age in this country. You see pensions and investments are taxed as "unearned income" and that leaves very little of them. It will be a pretty tough job translating a French book with no more knowledge of French than a dictionary can give! I don't see how any dictionary will enable one to understand a phrase like *est ce qu'il y en avait*. Get the French translation of some book you have in English (say the Bible) and try to get the hang of the language from that. Or perhaps the French *Lion, Witch, W.*,[1] which I enclose, would be more up to date and idiomatic. Between ourselves, I don't think you'll translate your present book very well, but you'll learn quite a lot of French in struggling with it and then your next attempt might be good. I wish I could relieve any of your various troubles—but it is very clear that the Holy Ghost is leading you through them all. With every blessing.

Yours
Jack Lewis

Magdalen
Nov 1st 54

Dear Mary

If you tell me that you don't know French, of course I believe you! If you were only coying and found my literal acceptance of the statement a shock—well, it'll "larn you" to practice mock modesty another time. It never works with me, I assure you. If a man tells me he can't do something I always believe him: *he* ought to know! I am very sorry to hear you have been ill. You don't give me any idea what the "old trouble" is. Anyway, I hope it has stood off again.

---

[1] *Le Lion et la Sorcière Blanche*, the French translation of Lewis's *The Lion, the Witch and the Wardrobe*.

About copies of the *Lion et la Sorcière* I presume the price and publisher's name and address are printed in the one you have, and an order to that publisher enclosing the requisite sum will elicit the goods! (People so often ask me how to get a book, and it seems an odd question. Are they equally puzzled how to order a cwt. of coals or a bottle of gin?). . . . No, my rheumatism is not really bad. It only produces extreme footsoreness in the left foot, so that after 50 yards, tho' the right one is fresh as a daisy the left keeps on whimpering "Stop! Stop! We've been 25 miles already." The real nuisance is that I am beginning to get horribly fat and this foot comes just when I ought to be slimming by long walks. I have had to give up potatoes, milk, and bread: perhaps having to fast for medical reasons is a just punishment for not having fasted enough on higher grounds! Did I tell you I've been made a professor at Cambridge? I take up my duties on Jan. 1st at Magdalene College, Cambridge (Eng.). Note the difference in spelling. It means rather less work for rather more pay. And I think I shall like Magdalene better than Magdalen. It's a tiny college (a perfect cameo architecturally) and they're all so old fashioned, and pious, and gentle and conservative—unlike this leftist, atheist, cynical, hard-boiled, huge Magdalen. Perhaps from being the fogey and "old woman" here I shall become the *enfant terrible* there. It is nice to be still under the care of St. Mary Magdalene: she must by now understand my constitution better than a stranger would, don't you think. The allegorical sense of her great action dawned on me the other day. The precious alabaster box which one must *break* over the Holy Feet is one's *heart*. Easier said than done. And the contents become perfume only when it is broken. While they are safe inside they are more like sewage. All very alarming.

> Yours
> Jack

> Magdalen College,
> Oxford
> Nov 17, 54

Dear Mary

No time to write properly but just a line to thank you for two letters. There is no need to apologise for your joke about the French: its only fault, as a joke, is that it is a bit *complicated!* Neuralgia in the ear is an old friend of mine and I think it usually comes from a draught. All blessings.

> Yours
> Jack

> Magdalen College
> Oxford
> Nov 20 54

Dear Mary

Thanks for the magazine. I think your "Pome" gets the awe and rigidity of the Byzantine atmosphere very well. As for McCarthy I never met anyone, American or English, who did not speak of him with horror. A very intelligent American pupil said "He is our potential Hitler".

> In haste.
> Yours
> Jack

Dear Mary

Yes, I've been treating you (and others) badly of
late, but, I think, with some excuse. First there were
visitors; then the preparations for the move; then the
move itself (at which moment my brother got ill so
that I had all the correspondence to tackle single
handed); then the settling in at Cambridge *plus* various delights like burst water-pipes; repeated journeys
to and fro—in fact a period during which life seemed
to consist entirely of journeys and letter writing—the
pen has become to me what the oar is to a galley
slave; then (God be praised) influenza and long half-
comatose days in bed. Yesterday was my first day
out. I hope to go back to work and Cambridge on
Thursday next. So I was about as likely to ride in a
steeplechase as to write a poem! But you have never
been absent from my prayers. So try not to be hurt by
my silence. And always remember that there is no
time in the whole year when I am less willing to
write than near Christmas, for it is then that my
burden is heaviest. I suspect you have a very false
idea of what my days are like! I am truly sorry about
your "physical difficulties" and hope the "examination" (always a horrid thing, whether scholastic, medical, or police!) is now all *happily* over. And now, you
really must forgive me: as you see, I can hardly form
the letters legibly! God bless you.

Yours
Jack

As from Magdalen College,
Cambridge
20/2/55

Dear Mary

Thanks for your letter of 14th. But why on earth didn't you write it a day later and tell me the result of the examination? I don't think we ought to try to keep up our normal prayers when we are ill and over-tired. I would not say this to a beginner who still has the habit to form. But you are past that stage. One mustn't make the Christian life into a punctilious system of *law*, like the Jewish [for] two reasons (1) It raises scruples when we don't keep the routine (2) It raises presumption when we do. Nothing gives one a more spuriously good conscience than keeping rules, even if there has been a total absence of all real charity and faith. And people who stay away from Mass with the approval of their director and at the bidding of their doctor are just as obedient as those who go. Check all these points with your confessor: I bet he'll say just the same. And of course the presence of God is not the same as the *sense* of the presence of God. The latter may be due to imagination; the former may be attended with no "sensible consolation". The Father was not *really* absent from the Son when He said "Why hast thou forsaken me?" You see God Himself, as man, submitted to man's sense of being abandoned. The real parallel on the natural level is one which seems odd for a bachelor to write to a lady, but too illuminating not to be used. The act which engenders a child ought to be, and usually is attended by pleasure. But it is not the pleasure that produces the child. Where there is pleasure there may be sterility: where there is no pleasure the act may be fertile. And in the spiritual marriage of God and the soul it is the same. It is the actual presence, not the *sensation* of the presence, of the Holy Ghost which begets Christ in us. The *sense* of the presence is a super-added gift for which we give thanks when it comes, and that's all about it. I am very sorry you are so overworked. Thanks for the review of Griffiths' book which I have of course read and enjoyed already. And I'm so pleased about the *Abolition of Man*, for it is almost my favorite among my books but in general has been almost totally ignored by the public. Give my love to Fanda: I am very "cat-minded". And always, let us pray for one another.

Yours
Jack

The Kilns
Kiln Lane
Headington Quarry
Oxford, England
21/3/55

Dear Mary

Thanks for your letter of the 16th. I am indeed sorry to hear of all the shocking things that have been happening to you. The bright spot is the result of the physical examination: there is one thing off your mind for good. I get the impression, not only from you but from many other correspondents, that in your country people are far too medically minded: they read and think too much about health and go to doctors too often! It seems to me crazy ever to have an operation unless it is either a quite trivial one or quite clearly necessary. My own doctor, who happened to be also one of my most intimate friends (he's a R.C.) says that the vast majority of illnesses are either incurable or (which is fortunately the larger class) cure themselves in due course. I said "But my cough *does* get better after I've been taking cough mixture for a day or two". He replied "Yes, because you don't start the mixture until the cough has become a real nuisance, which means until it was reaching its peak after which it would have gone away in about the same time whether you had taken the mixture or not". A good deal of your alarming story I didn't understand. Why is cutting off one's telephone a protection against assault? It sounds to me just as much a *non-sequitur* as going armed in the streets to protect one-self from the telephone calls! But of course the thing itself is no joke and you must be badly shaken: I hope you feel better now. We were talking about cats and dogs the other day and decided that both have con-sciences but the dog, being an honest, humble person, always has a bad one, but the cat is a Pharisee and always has a good one. When he sits and stares you out of countenance he is thanking God that he is not as these dogs, or these humans, or even as these other cats! I'm sending this by air mail because you en-closed stamps. But the stamps are, you know, quite useless here, and in future I'll continue to send by surface mail. Postage is rather a serious item in my weekly budget. In great haste—I hope it is legible—and with all sympathy and blessings. *Oremus pro invicem* as you people say.

Yours
Jack

The Kilns, etc
24/3/55

Dear Mary

Just a line of sympathy and encouragement on the impending operation. Extra faith has been given to meet crises before, and I pray that it will be now. Be very much on guard against the growth of a feeling that Fr.A. or anyone else "Does not sound interested".

When we are in trouble we easily think this, don't we? And at all times, we very easily misinterpret expressions of face and tones of voice. Often, too, the person we speak to is at that moment full of troubles we know nothing about. Fr. D'Arcy and I were both members of the Dante Society at one time and I have also spoken on the same platform, so I know him pretty well. He is a most interesting man and an excellent speaker.

My prayers always,
Yours
Jack

The Kilns, etc
2nd April 1955.

Dear Mary

In great haste. I hope your next letter will bring me news that the operation has gone swimmingly. Fear is horrid, but there's no reason to be ashamed of it. Our Lord was afraid (dreadfully so) in Gethsemane. I always cling to that as a very comforting fact. All blessings.

Yours,
Jack

The Kilns, etc
8/5/55

Dear Mary

I am extremely sorry (and at such a time too) to have left your letter of April 14th so long unanswered. But there was a chapter of obstacles. First, you put no address on the letter and the outside of the envelope had got damp so that the address was illegible. Second, I was in Cambridge (where your letter was forwarded) and your address in the files here. Thirdly, my brother was away ill, so that I couldn't send mine to him to be addressed. Fourthly, there was a railway strike which prevented me coming home last week-end as I would normally have done. That brings us to yesterday!

I'm glad the operation is over, and sorry about the sinus headaches (an enemy of mine for some years now). But I prefer them to sick headaches all the same: they're a "clean pain" and don't entail the same *general* malaise—what someone I knew called "the all-overish feeling". How nice all that is about the "efficient" young woman you were able to help. I *think* I know what you mean by the "humiliation" of finding everyone much nicer to one than seemed probable beforehand. It is a very gentle, pleasant kind, though, isn't it? (There are others! By gum, aren't there?). I like the second stanza of *Easter* best. Between ourselves, as one rhymester to another, it's a great pity that *world*, such a good important word and often so emphatically demanding to come at the end of a line, has so few rhymes in English. *Furled, hurled, curled*—none of them very serviceable—and what else is there. Let's invent a verb *to churl* (behave churlishly).

This is the coldest spring ever in England, and I have hardly heard the cuckoo at all till (when I didn't specially want him) 5 a.m. this morning.

You are always in my prayers: have me in yours.

Yours
Jack

The Kilns, etc
14/5/55

Dear Mary

Thanks for yours of the 8th. I hope you now have a letter of mine, explaining my involuntary silence. Here's the lecture: a dull work, except for the special

audience I had in view.[1] I heard *Time* had been at
me (Time, in another sense always is!) but didn't see
it. I'm glad you had such a nice birthday party; not
that I'm fond of birthday parties myself. You don't say
exactly how you are, but I hope no news is good
news. All good wishes.

> Yours in haste
> Jack

[1] Perhaps a reference to his inaugural lecture at Cambridge, *De Descriptione Temporum.*

> Magdalene College
> Cambridge
> 7/6/55

Dear Mary

Thanks for your letter of the 29th. The photo from
Time was a useful mortification; good as a hair shirt.
(What an exaggeration! as if one wouldn't rather look
like the Ugly Duchess than wear even ordinary tickly
underclothing for half a day!) I think all your activities as fairy-godmother to a Chinese bride must be
delightful, and you obviously find them so. It's a little
alarming to hear that she doesn't want to marry anyone. But I daresay she'll feel differently when she's
had a baby. But of course the whole Chinese set-up is
quite different, isn't it? With them (I understand)
parents are everything, and one's husband (still more,
one's wife) is nothing. I'm shocked to find that a shop
wouldn't serve a Chinese. But I have long known that
the talk about Brotherhood, wherever it occurs, in
America or here, is hypocrisy. Or rather, the man who
talks it means 'I have no superiors': he does *not* mean
'I have no inferiors'. How loathsome it all is!

The warm weather (what we call warm here) has
begun at last and the cuckoo is at his work. I had my
first bathe two days ago. Meanwhile the railway

strike (there's Brotherhood and Democracy for you again) goes on. I'm going to try to travel to Oxford on Saturday, but it is a mere adventure. My whitening bones will probably be found by the wayside.

All good wishes and blessings.

Yours
Jack

Magdalene College
Cambridge
21/6/55

Dear Mary

Thanks for the cutting. It does seem rum to be afraid of the Confessional and then send off your whole story to be printed in a newspaper! (You don't think some of these letters are really written in the editor's office: a pious fraud for instructional purposes?). I'm sorry about your two jealous colleagues. I suppose the only way with thorns in the flesh (until one can get them out) is not to press on the place where they are embedded; i.e. to stop one's thoughts (firmly but gently: no good snapping at oneself, it only increases the fuss—read St. François de Sales' chapter on Meekness toward oneself) whenever one finds them moving towards the unpleasant people. . . .

The pen doesn't lure me on as the typewriter, you say, lures you! So I must stop. All good wishes.

Yours
Jack

The Kilns, etc
30/6/55

Dear Mary

In great haste. It wasn't a battle I had; only a bathe—my bad writing again. About prides, superiorities, and affronts there's no book better than Law's

Serious Call to a Devout and Holy Life where you'll
find all of us pinned like butterflies on cards—the
cards being little stories of typical characters in the
most sober, astringent 18th century prose. Now for
my train—I have to go to London for two nights.

Yours
Jack

Magdalene College,
Cambridge
5/10/55

Dear Mary

I have just got your letter of Oct. 1st. I don't know
quite what has happened, and it is possible a letter
may have gone astray. I didn't think I was so far
behindhand. (You have, you know, recently stepped
up the pace of the correspondence! I can't play at
that tempo, you know). I thought I had sent you a
copy of my new book, *Surprised by Joy*. But that can
be remedied when I'm back in Oxford this week end.
I was there most of the vacation and then for a
fortnight or so in Ireland:—Donegal, which is a most
heavenly place. I found my brother ill when I got
home and so lacked his usual secretarial help, so that
for a while life seemed to consist almost entirely of
letter writing—I wonder how many people besides
you I have failed to answer! I am now, as you see,
back in Cambridge, where the marvellous summer (I
remember only one other so hot and dry in my life) is
still going on, or only turning deliciously into still,
misty, voluptuous autumn. I am sorry you tell me so
little about yourself in your letter, for even when I
don't write I pray. . . . You have no idea how many
instances of domestic nastiness come before me in my
mail: how deceptive the smooth surface of life is! The
only "ordinary" homes seem to be the ones we don't

know much about, just as the only blue mountains are those 10 miles away. And now, I really *must* tackle the remaining letters. With all good wishes.

Yours
Jack Lewis

As from Magdalene,
Cambridge
9/10/55

Dear Mary

I've just got your letter from the 3rd. and am glad to find that the book has arrived; not least because it saves me doing one of the things which (in a small way) I dislike most in the world: putting up a Parcel. Thanks also for the almost scandalously munificent gift of stamps. But (seriously) never do it again. Stamps are money, and you have none to spare. I envy your friends their 12 acre tract of woodland but should loathe a house that is nearly all glass. Not (I think) because I'm very fond of throwing stones, but I like to feel in-doors when I'm in. The main charm of the view from a room is the fact that it is framed in, and unified by, the window. And I hate indoor sunlight. It makes shadows across the page of your book and turns the print green. All really open-air people (sailors, and farm labourers) like thick walls, small windows, and those *shut!* I couldn't agree with you more about games; but—dare I confess it?—I feel just the same about furs. I like them *on* the beasts of course. I am sorry the trials come so thick and fast, but glad you should be so supported by Our dear Lord. All blessings.

Yours
Jack Lewis

Magdalene College,
Cambridge.
26/10/55

Dear Mary

I have your letter of Oct. 21, and do feel the deepest sympathy for all your complication of troubles. Your dentist, I feel, ought to go to jail. I never heard (in modern times) of such an operation being done without anaesthetics. Here, you'd get it free. I didn't quite understand the bit about the hypodermic nor what is the suspected cause of the pains. The anxiety about the future is, however, a thing we can all understand, and *very* hard to bear. You were almost miraculously supported in such anxiety before and I pray you may be now. And I think it is happening. Your faith is a support to me as well as to yourself. But how one even *ought* to feel—let alone, how one can succeed in feeling—about——is a problem. It is very hard to believe that all one's indignation is simply bad: but I suppose one must stick to the text "The wrath of *man* worketh not the righteousness of *God*", I suppose one must keep on remembering that there is always something deeply wrong inside with a man so bad as this. For yourself I can only hope—and passages in your letter confirm my hope—that through all this you are being brought closer to God than you could have been otherwise. And it is not forever (wouldn't it be ghastly to be *immortal* on earth, like the Wandering Jew?). It will all one day go away like a dream.

The only reason I'm *not* sick of all the stuff about ——is that I don't read it. I never read the papers. Why does anyone? They're nearly all lies, and one has to wade thru' such reams of verbiage and "write up" to find out even what they're saying.

Well, must stop. Ten letters this morning and (one

can't get breakfast till 8.30 here) it's now 11.25. Not a stroke of my own work done and all the cream of the day gone. God bless and keep you.

Yours
Jack

As from Magdalene,
Cambridge
9/11/55

Dear Mary

Thanks for yours of the 3rd and very kind review.[1] Kind, but not *quite* accurate when you say I met "joy" in the "whimsical creations of my boyish imagination". Surely the book tells you very explicitly that I never met it *there*? But no matter. You give the core of it very well and with great economy and clarity: a good bit of work.

How it bucks one up to get a poem accepted! the children we are. I look forward to your article.

I agree: the only thing one can usually change in one's situation is oneself. And yet one can't change that either—only ask Our Lord to do so, keeping on meanwhile with one's sacraments, prayers, and ordinary rule of life. One mustn't fuss too much about one's state. Do you read St. Francis de Sales? He has good things to say on this subject. All good wishes.

Yours
Jack Lewis

The Kilns,
Headington Quarry
16/12/55

Dear Mary

I was most distressed by the news in your letter of Dec. 2d. It was touching the way you spent the first

[1] Of Lewis's autobiography *Surprised by Joy*.

page telling me nice things about my own books and
... then disclosed your own great trouble at the end.
And I can't help you, because under the modern laws
I'm not allowed to send money to America. (What a
barbarous system we live under. I knew a man who
had to risk *prison* in order to smuggle a little money
to his own sister, widowed in U.S.A.). By the way, we
mustn't be too sure there was any irony about your
just having refused that other job. There may have
been a snag about it which God knew and you didn't.

I feel it almost impossible to say anything (in my
comfort and security—apparent security, for real security is in Heaven and thus earth affords only imita-
tions) which would not sound horribly false and fac-
ile. Also, you know it all better than I do. I should in
your place be (I *have* in similar places *been*) far
more panic-stricken and even perhaps rebellious. For
it is a dreadful truth that the state of (as you say)
"having to depend solely on God" is what we all
dread most. And of course that just shows how very
much, how almost exclusively, we have been depend-
ing on things. But trouble goes so far back in our
lives and is now so deeply ingrained, we *will* not turn
to Him as long as He leaves us anything else to turn to.
I suppose all one can say is that it was bound to
come. In the hour of death and the day of judgment,
what else shall we have? Perhaps when those moments come, they will feel happiest who have been
forced (however unwittingly) to begin practising it
here on earth. It is good of Him to *force* us; but dear
me, how hard to *feel* that it is good at the time.

The little Christmas poem was nice. I particularly
liked "The curtain spread By the simplicity around"—
a very precise idea economically expressed.

All's well—I'm half ashamed it should be—with me. God bless and keep you. You shall be constantly in my prayers by day and night.

Yours
Jack Lewis

The Kilns etc.
19/12/55

Dear Mary

Thanks for your letter of Dec. 15. I don't see anything wrong with the way in which you tell your story ... wrong in the stylistic way, I mean. You have made it sound at one point as if Episcopalians didn't think suicide a sin! But no doubt that is unintentional. I think the narrative good.

I do hope you will get the nicer of those two jobs, which is certainly the one I also would prefer in your place. Not of course that one can be sure what either is like till one has got inside. Things turn out both so much [better] and so much worse than they look, don't they? Be sure you remain very much in my thoughts and prayers.

I seem to have been writing Christmas letters most of this day! I'm afraid I hate the weeks just before Christmas, and so much of the (very commercialised and vulgarised) fuss has nothing to do with the Nativity at all. I wish we didn't live in a world where buying and selling things (especially selling) seems to have become almost more important than either producing or using them.

All blessings. "Beneath are the everlasting arms" even when it doesn't feel at all like it.

Yours
Jack Lewis

Magdalene College,
Cambridge
8/2/56

Dear Mary

Thanks for your letter of the 2d and for the *Time*
cutting. My brother says the photo of me is the best
ever, but another friend says it is unrecognisable.
What's most impressive is the smoke from the match,[1]
which looks like the explosion of a miniature shell.
The review is of course a tissue of muddles and direct
falsehoods—I don't say "lies" because the people who
write such things are not really capable of lying. I
mean, to lie = to say what you know to be untrue.
But to know this, and to have the very ideas of truth
and falsehood in your head, presupposes a clarity of
mind which they haven't got. To call them liars
would be as undeserved a compliment as to say that
a dog was bad at arithmetic.

I am delighted to hear that the new job continues
to give satisfaction. What a difference it makes to
work with nice people and to do work that you can
believe in.

We have just come through a spell of what we call
hard frost. It would be nothing by American standards: but here all the pipes burst and electricity and
gas go down to low pressure, so one is comfortless
enough.

You are still always in my prayers.

Yours
Jack Lewis

[1] A picture of Lewis as he was lighting his pipe.

Dear Mary

I thought the boot was on the other foot and that I had in fact written to you since you wrote to me—congratulating you on the new job which seemed such an answer to your prayers and those of your friends.

Well, what is my news? A good deal of it is probably not interesting. I was very excited by seeing a performance of the *Bacchae*, but Greek plays aren't up your street. I've just been in Edinburgh to speak at the annual dinner of the Walter Scott Club:[1] but unless you happen to be a reader of Scott there's no point in telling you that the Provost of Edinburgh (who sat next me) was *exactly* like Bailie Nichol Jarvie out of *Rob Roy*. The Scotch run awfully true to type and never change. Edinburgh is a wonderful city, with a castle on a crag and mountains beyond it all visible from the main street. (I imagine Quebec being a bit like it, but I may be all wrong). We've lived thro' 3 weeks (for us) very severe frost, but to-day is the first of spring: warm sunshine, pure blue sky, and all the birds singing like mad. My new book went to press last week.[2] It is the story of Cupid and Psyche told by one of the sisters—so that I believe I've done what no mere male author has done before, talked thro' the mouth of, and lived in the mind of, an *ugly* woman for a whole book. All female readers so far have approved the feminine psychology of it: i.e. no masculine note intrudes. I think that's about all

---

[1] See "Sir Walter Scott," in Lewis's *They Asked for a Paper*.
[2] *Till We Have Faces*.

that has happened to me. This is the eighth letter this (Sunday) morning. What Sabbath-breach!

I hope all continues to go well.

Yours sincerely
Jack Lewis

The Kilns,
Headington Quarry,
Oxford
19/3/56

Dear Mary

A line in haste about the bits underlined in your letter (which I enclose for reference). Don't be too easily convinced that God really wants you to do all sorts of work you needn't do. Each must do his duty "in that state of life to which God has called him". Remember that a belief in the virtues of doing for doing's sake is characteristically feminine, characteristically American, and characteristically modern: so that *three* veils may divide you from the correct view! There can be intemperance in work just as in drink. What feels like zeal may be only fidgets or even the flattering of one's self-importance. As MacDonald says "In holy things may be unholy greed". And by doing what "one's station and its duties" does not demand, one can make oneself less fit for the duties it *does* demand, one can make oneself less fit for the duties it *does* demand and so commit some injustice. Just you give Mary a little chance as well as Martha!

Yours
Jack

Dear Mary

I don't know what "high-hatting" means, but it is in this country a safe bet that 999 out of a 1000 people have no use for Scott; and the more high-brow they are, the safer. He is despised by everyone (except a few old fogies like myself) in England. I didn't say "great plays", I said GREEK plays (this is the trouble about my handwriting). It is not offensive to assume that a lady doesn't read Greek—not even in a University town! And I have no "cultural activities". I like the *Bacchae* because it's exciting, not because it is —loathsome word!—"cultured". In fact, you misunderstood my letter.

All the best.

Yours
Jack

Dear Mary

Thank you for your letter of the 31st and for the enclosed poem, which I enjoyed. I think it brings all the threads together well. The complexity—the close texture—of all the great events in the Christian year impresses me more and more. Each is a window opening on the total mystery.

I sympathise with you for the unnamed shock you speak of, without the least inquisitiveness as to its nature; being sure your own decision (not to tell it) was right. Except when speaking to one's Confessor,

Doctor, or Lawyer (where the opposite holds) I suppose the rule is "When in doubt, don't tell". At least I have nearly always regretted doing the opposite and never once regretted holding my tongue. (Talking too much is one of my vices, by the way).

About prayer (for others) and suffering for others there's a lot scattered through 2d Corinthians which is well worth meditation.

The reviews of *S. by J.*[1] (Don't bother sending them—I get them) *are* funny. The sheer errors of fact—not to go into misunderstandings—would ruin a candidate in the most elementary exam I know!

The spring *looks* lovely thru' windows here but remains bitterly cold. I go back to Cambridge the day after tomorrow.

All blessings.

> Yours
> Jack

> Magdalene College,
> Cambridge.
> 26/4/56

Dear Mary

I am most sorry to hear about your recent experiences. Though I am not doctor enough nor psychologist enough to understand them, I can see that they must have been very unpleasant indeed. You may be very sure of my continued, and increased, prayers. One of the many reasons for wishing to be a better Christian is that, if one were, one's prayers for others might be more effectual. Things do come all together and so quickly in life, don't they? Of course we have all been taught what to do with suffering—offer it in Christ to God as our little, little share of Christ's sufferings—but it is so hard to do. I am afraid I can

[1] *Surprised by Joy.*

better imagine, than *really* enter into, this. I suppose that if one loves a person enough one would actually wish to share every part of his life; and I suppose the great saints thus really *want* to share the divine sufferings and that is how they can actually desire pain. But this is far beyond me. To grin and bear it and (in some feeble, desperate way) to *trust* is the utmost most of us can manage. One tries to take a lesson not only from the saints but from the beasts: how well a sick dog trusts one if one has to do things that hurt it! And this, I know, in some measure you will be able to do.

Well, I hope your next news will be better. Meanwhile, may Our Lord support you as only He can.

Yours
Jack

Magdalene College,
Cambridge
21/5/56

Dear Mary

What a horrid adventure. To meet unrestrained anger in any human being is in itself always very shocking. I think the effect may be partly physical. Have you noticed how *one* angry man bursts out (say, in a crowded 'bus) and a tension comes over everyone? Indeed one nearly becomes equally angry oneself. When one gets this shock along with injustice of course there is a compound reaction. It is at first sight so easy to forgive (especially when one knows that the anger was pathological) but then one sort of wakes up five minutes later and finds one hasn't really forgiven at all—the resentment is still tingling thro' one's veins. And how one has to watch that "feeling hurt"—so seldom (as one would like to believe) mere sorrow, so nearly always mixed with

wounded pride, self-justification, fright, even (hiding
in the corners) desire for retaliation. But obviously
you know all this and have fought your best. But
there remains the quite separate trouble of having
lost your job. Oh dear. I *am* sorry. Surely all these
Church people will find some way to provide for you.
I will indeed pray—oh, what a business life is. Well,
both you and I have most of it behind, not ahead.
There will come a moment that will change all this.
Nightmares don't last.

Yours
Jack

The Kilns,
Headington Quarry,
Oxford
14/6/56

Dear Mary

I have your letter of the 11th—along with a letter
from another lady in almost exactly the same position. Oh dear, what a hard, frightening world it is!
And yet not wholly; I am rejoiced to hear that you
have some true friends who will not let you sink. And
why should there be any (let alone "too much")
"cringing inside"? We are all members of one another
and must all learn to receive as well as to give. I am
only sorry that the laws[1] prevent me from giving you
any lessons in the art. Isn't the spiritual value of
having to accept money just this, that it makes palpa-
ble the total dependence in which we always live
anyway? For if you were what is called "independent" (i.e. living on inherited wealth) every bit you
put into your mouth and every stitch on your back
would still be coming from the sweat and skill of

[1] He means that the English legal system prevents him from
sending her money.

others while you (as a person) would not really be doing anything in return. It took me a long time to see this—tho', heaven knows, with the Cross before our eyes we have little excuse to forget our insolvency.

The great thing with unhappy times is to take them bit by bit, hour by hour, like an illness. It is seldom the *present*, the exact present, that is unbearable.

I shall pray for you whenever I wake in the night, and hope for better news.

Yours
Jack Lewis

The Kilns,
Headington Quarry,
Oxford
5/7/56

Dear Mary

Thank you for your letter of June 30th. Yes, what your Franciscan author says is very true. As some one says "The Devil used to try to prevent people from doing good works, but he has now learned a trick worth two of that: he *organises* 'em instead".

I am very, very glad that God has sent you good friends who won't let you sink, and that you have turned the corner about that bad feeling that one must not take help even when one needs it. If it were really true that to receive money or money's worth degraded the recipient, then every act of alms we have done in our lives would be wicked! Dives was quite right to leave Lazarus lying at his gate! Or else (which might be even worse) we should have to hold that to receive was good enough for those we call "the poor" but not for our precious selves however poor we become! How difficult it is to avoid having a special standard for oneself! DeQuincey says somewhere that probably no murderer mentally describes his own act by the word *murder*; and how many people in the whole world believe themselves to be snobs, prigs, bores, bullies or tale-bearers? Talking of murder, do you see we're abolishing capital punishment in this country? Do you think we're wise or foolish? . . .

I'm very busy with preparing lectures. This is the most sunless summer I ever remember.

> Yours
> Jack

> The Kilns,
> Headington Quarry,
> Oxford
> 3/8/56

Dear Mary

I have your letter of July 30th and am very sorry to hear that you are still in difficulties. Your "pleasures" (i.e. social engagements) seem to be almost as much of an affliction as anything else!—but I can understand that. . . . I think what one has to remember when people "hurt" one is that in 99 cases out of a 100 they intended to hurt very much less, or not at all, and are often quite unconscious of the whole thing. I've learned this from the cases in which I was the "hurter". When I have been really wicked and angry and meant to be nasty the other party never cared or even didn't notice. On the other hand, when I have found out afterwards that I had deeply hurt someone, it had nearly always been quite unconscious on my part. (I *loathe* "sensitive" people who are "easily hurt" by the way, don't you? They are a social pest. Vanity is usually the real trouble).

I read *Don Camillo* some years ago, but can't imagine how it could be made into a film. I suppose they drag some love story into it? (But then I'm, as you know, rather allergic to the films).

I have known nice (and nasty) Hindoos. I should have thought the nice ones were precisely "Pagans", if one uses *Pagan* not in the popular modern sense—which means pretty nearly "irreligious",—but strictly. I.e., I think all that extreme refinement and that spirituality which takes the form of despising matter, is very like Pythagoras and Plato and Marcus Aurelius. Poor dears: they don't know about the Sacraments nor the resurrection of the body.

Yes, I know how terrible that doubt is "Perhaps He will not". But it is so seldom the present and the actual that is intolerable. Remember one is given strength to bear what happens to one, but not the 100 and 1 different things that *might* happen. And don't say God has proved that *He* can *make you fear* poverty, illness, etc. I am sure God never teaches us the fear of anything but Himself. As the only two good lines in one of our bad hymns says "Fear Him ye saints and you will then have nothing else to fear". (Racine, no doubt independently has the same thing in *Athalie—je crains Dieu et n'ai pas d'autre crainte*). Not all the things you fear can happen to you; the one (if any) that does will perhaps turn out very different from what you think. Of course I know this is easier to say to another than to realise oneself. And always remember that poverty and every other ill, lovingly accepted, has all the spiritual value of voluntary poverty or penance. God bless you; you are always in my prayers.

Yours
Jack

Somewhere in Eire
18/8/56

Dear Mary

It's no good giving you an address for I am moving

about. Your letter of Aug. 12th reached me today. I am delighted to hear about the job. It sounds exactly the thing, sent by God, at your most need. I will never laugh at anyone for grieving over a loved beast. I think God wants us to love Him *more*, not to love creatures (even animals) *less*. We love everything in *one* way too much (i.e. at the expense of our love for Him) but in another way we love everything too little.

No person, animal, flower, or even pebble, has ever been loved too much—i.e. more than every one of God's works deserves. But you need not feel "like a murderer". Rather rejoice that God's law allows you to extend to Fanda that last mercy which (no doubt, quite rightly) we are forbidden to extend to suffering humans. You'll get over this. . . .

I'm writing on a dressing table in a small, dark hotel bed-room, very sleepy, so I'll close. God bless you—and Fanda!

Yours
Jack Lewis

Drumbeg Hotel,
Inver,
Co. Donegal
Sept. 8/56

Dear Mary

I can't quite understand all the affair about the Bank, being intensely stupid about everything that might be called business—but perhaps for that very reason all the more able to enter into your dismay. All that side of life is to me simply a terrifying mystery. But I hope I am right in thinking that it all turned out well in the end. It certainly looks as if God were looking after you financially. I expect that the instruments He uses are kind human beings: and all the better if so, for then it is good for them as well as for you.

How charming about your young friend and her present!

I used to meet Fr. D'Arcy pretty often when he was Master of Campion Hall, for we were both members of the Dante Society. Remember me to him if you happen to meet him.

I think what I must have said about Hindus (but can I write it any more legibly *this* time?) was that, if you use *Pagan* in the proper sense, i.e. to mean Polytheist, then they are Pagans, but not of course if you use that word in the journalists' sense, to mean "irreligious" or even "debauched" (that journalists can be saved is a doctrine, if not contrary to, yet certainly above, reason!).

I am glad you like my stories. They are the part of my work I like best.

It continues cold (you would think it Arctic) here and wet, but with lovely gleams at times in which far-off mountains show three times their real height and with a radiance that suggests Bunyan's "delectable mountains".

I hope your health will soon improve.

Yours

Jack Lewis

P.S.—I doubt if you'll find any Leprechauns in Eire now. The Radio has driven them away.

Royal Port Hotel,
Rathmullen
Co. Donegal,
EIRE
Sept. 14 [1956]

Thanks for cutting containing yourself and Sister Mary Frances and Mr. Birch and me; both interesting. Problem: why are nuns nicer than monks and schoolgirls nicer than schoolboys, when women are not in general nicer than men? But perhaps you deny all three statements!

All blessings.

J

The Kilns
Headington Quarry
Oxford, England
20 Oct/56

Dear Mary

I can't answer yours of the 14th as it deserves for it comes to me on a day when I am all embroiled with affairs arising out of a friend's sudden illness, and very much distressed. Alas, troubles everywhere. . . . I am very very sorry to hear about your health. "Hives on the eyes" must be horrid and go all through one's head. And the anxiety too. May God comfort you. I'm thankful He has at any rate given you some good friends.

In great haste.

Yours
Jack

Magdalene College,
Cambridge
Nov 16/56

Dear Mary

Very sorry to hear all your bad news. . . .

You may as well know (but don't talk of it, for all is still uncertain) that I may soon be, in rapid succession, a bridegroom and a widower. There may, in fact, be a deathbed marriage. I can hardly describe to you the state of mind I live in at present—except that all emotion, with me, is periodically drowned in sheer tiredness, deep lakes of stupour. Perhaps a very heavy cold in the head helps this. So you won't expect me to write long or many letters. Let us always pray for one another.

> Yours
> Jack

> The Kilns
> Headington Quarry
> Oxford, England
> Dec. 12th 1956

Dear Mary

I am sorry to hear that your news is still no better; but I don't somehow think that all your friends will leave you in the lurch if things come to the worst.

Why should I make a mystery of my own affairs? (but don't mention it till it becomes public). I am likely to be, in the near future, both a husband and a widower. That is, I am marrying a very sick, and perhaps a dying, woman. That's all.

We will keep one another in our prayers.

> Yours
> Jack

> The Kilns
> Headington Quarry
> Oxford, England
> 4/1/57

Dear Mary

Thank you for your letter of the 28th with enclosures. I must try not to let my own present unhappiness harden my heart against the woes of others! You too are going through a dreadful time. Ah well, it

will not last forever. There will come a day for all of
us when "it is finished". God help us all.

Yours sincerely
Jack

Magdalene College,
Cambridge
17/1/57

Dear Mary

I've got such an attack of rheumatism in my right
arm I can hardly write. I have married a lady suffering from cancer. I think she will weather it this time:
after that, life under the sword of Damocles. Very
little chance (not exactly *none*) of a permanent es-
cape. I acquire two schoolboy stepsons. My brother
and I have been coping with them for their Christmas
holidays. Nice boys, but gruelling work for 2 old
bachelors! I'm dead tired now.

Yours very sincerely
Jack Lewis

The Kilns
Headington Quarry
Oxford, England
17/2/57

Dear Mary

There is no great mystery about my marriage. I
have known the lady a long time: no one can mark
the exact moment at which friendship becomes love.
You can well understand how illness—the fact that
she was facing pain and death and anxiety about the
future of her children—would be an *extra* reason for
marrying her or a reason for marrying her sooner. If I
write very shortly it is not because I am reticent but
because I am tired and busy. My brother is also ill

and causes a good deal of anxiety, and of course I lose his secretarial help; so that I have not only much to bear but much to *do*. I can't type; you could hardly conceive what hundreds of hours a year I spend coaxing a rheumatic wrist to drive this pen across paper.

What a divine mercy about the last moment money for the rent! Clearly He who feeds the sparrows has you in His care. Never suppose that the amount "on my own plate" shuts up my sympathy for the great troubles you are undergoing. I pray for you every day. Ah well, we shall all be out of it in a comparatively few years. With blessings.

Yours
Jack Lewis

Magdalene College,
Cambridge
14/3/57

Dear Mary

I can't really write to-day but just send a line to thank you for your kind letter of March 8th. I am very glad to hear about the job or jobs. All much the same at this end.

Yours
Jack

The Kilns, Kiln Lane,
Headington Quarry,
Oxford.
13th April 1957.

Dear Mary

My wife is now home, bed-ridden, and dying. We have two nurses. You really must not expect more than notes from me. I lead the life of a hospital orderly, and have hardly time to say my prayers or eat my meals.

Thanks for the Easter poem, and congratulations on the job.

Yours,
Jack

The Kilns,
Headington Quarry,
Oxford
June 18th, 1957

Dear Mary

We go on. Joy is to all appearance (blessedly or heart-breakingly) well and anyone but a doctor would feel sure she was recovering.[1] My brother is well and very helpful. I have had and have some trouble in my back (perhaps I told you this before?) which produced a few muscle spasms and screams from me but is now only a wearisome ache. We have a heat wave. I heard from some one who knows you the other day—all about a rumour of my own death! I trust all goes well with you.

Yours
Jack Lewis

The Kilns etc.
July 3/57

Dear Mary

Thanks for letter. I fear I must be very brief. I am sorry to hear of your renewed trouble. Yes, my wife was Joy Davidman: I hope you've read her *Smoke on the Mountains*. What on earth is the trouble about there being a rumour of my death? There's nothing discreditable in dying: I've known the most respect-

[1] Cf. paragraph three of Lewis's essay "The Efficacy of Prayer." Also his letter of January 26, 1959.

able people do it! Joy is in no pain and in wonderful (apparent) health and spirits.

All good wishes.

Yours
Jack

The Kilns,
Headington Quarry,
Oxford
Aug 12th 1957

Dear Mary

Thanks for your kind letter of Aug. 8th. Of course I showed it to Joy who got great pleasure from it and sends you her love. I enclose both our autographs.

She continues (apparently) to mend—in fact (o irony!) her face now is that of a woman in better health than in the photo you have seen: much less drawn and intense and far livelier. (But of course no man ever approves the photos of the woman he loves!)

My *osteoporosis* doesn't seem to get much better, but at least it has never been so bad again as it was when it began. I'm wearing a Surgical Belt—very like one's grandmother's corsets. It gives me a wonderfully youthful figure. Both my stepsons are now home from school for the summer holidays. They are well and seem happy enough.

Even *our* heat wave was trying: *yours* must have been ghastly. I sympathise with you for that and all your other afflictions.

Yours
Jack

Dear Mary

We are shocked and distressed at the news in your letter of the 15th. I think I see from what you say that God is already giving you new spiritual strength with which to meet this terrible affliction—just as He did to us in Joy's worst times. But pain is pain. I wish I could relieve any of it for you—one is so ineffective. The great thing, as you have obviously seen, (both as regards pain and financial worries) is to live from day to day and hour to hour not adding the past or future to the present. As one lived in the Front Line "They're not shelling us at the moment, and it's not raining, and the rations have come up, so let's enjoy ourselves". In fact, as Our Lord said, "Sufficient unto the day". You may be sure you will be very much in our prayers. All my news is good, very good up-to-date, tho' of course we live always under the sword of Damocles. God bless and keep you, dear friend. It'll be nice when we all wake up from this life which has indeed something like nightmare about it.

Yours
Jack

Dear Mary

Oh what bad luck! Tooth troubles on top of all the rest. The financial side of it is probably really the least formidable. As our ancestors used to say, you have "lived at God's charges" so far, and no doubt He will continue to foot the bill. Nor do I think you are in the least danger of getting "queer"—except that we're all queer. We've been having influenza and the few days in bed seem (so odd is my complaint) to have done my bones harm—i.e. they're not so good as they were three weeks ago, but they're not so bad as they were 6 weeks ago. Joy continues to make progress. All blessings and sympathy.

Yours
Jack

As from Magdalene College,
Cambridge
Nov. 30th 1957

Dear Mary

Thanks for your letter of Nov. 22d. Yes: moves are desolating things. The wind of Time blows cold at these corners, doesn't it?—and one's belongings have a sort of squalid pathos about them once they are packed. But one often feels better afterwards and I hope you will find this. Of course the new home is a tiring nuisance until the new ways which it demands have become habits. After that, it may begin to have a certain rejuvenating quality. You don't mention the heart-trouble: I hope that means you are feeling a great deal better.

All goes wonderfully well with Joy; we are very blessed at present. My own bone disease (osteoporosis) will, I gather, be always with me, but I am not in a painful condition now. I'll never be able to take real walks again—field-paths and little woods and wonderful inns in remote villages, farewell!—but it's wonderful how mercifully the desire goes when the power goes.

With all good wishes.

Yours
Jack

70

Dear Mary

Your letter reached me before I left home this morning on my way back to college, this being the first day of term. I came by car (hired) and Joy came with me for the drive and went home after lunch. It sounds a small thing, but it would have been incredible even a month ago.

I am sorry you have been having trouble with your cat. We (have) had a rather "animallic" time for our old bitch (we thought she knew better) made us an unexpected Christmas present of 10 puppies! We are tired of hearing neighbours say "Oh, thank you—we'd *love* a puppy, but—"

The worst of all economies is on necessary medicines, tho' I quite understand how you are tempted to it. What a pity you haven't got our National Health system in America. I wish I could help. I can only continue my prayers. My bones, by the way, are quite quiescent, so I don't need to be pitied. God has been wonderfully good to us in every way.

Forgive my awful hand and short letters—both have the same cause. This is the 8th letter (all by hand) and the end is not yet! God bless you, and guard you from all danger.

Yours sincerely
C. S. Lewis

As from Magdalene College
Cambridge
22/2/58

Dear Mary

Joy (who thanks you for your most kind message) tells me I am writing to you on George Washington's birthday, so "there's glory for you" as Humpty Dumpty would say. God is very good to us and we go on happily at present. We kept one of the puppies, and call him Guppy (out of *Bleak House*) and he is a lively youngster. I notice, as I have done before in similar circumstances, the common *age* is a bond stronger than common species; i.e. Guppy is friends with the kitten and Guppy's mother is friends with the old cat—a huge Tom called Ginger. I'm glad my angels should be thought more correct than those of the "Repository Artists", but what the dickens *are* Repository Artists? I never heard of them.

I am sorry you had such a bad time at the dentist's but hope that the total result is an improvement. Your mention of "Valentines" carried me back many years: I have not seen one since I was a small boy, as they have almost died out in this country.

Yes, we must not fret about not doing God those supposed services which He in fact does not allow us to do. Very often I expect, the service He really demands is that of *not* being (apparently) used, or not in the way we expected, or not in a way we can perceive.

I've written an article for an American magazine called *The Christian Herald*.[1]

With all good wishes and love from us both.

Yours
Jack

---

[1] "Shall We Lose God in Outer Space?"

Dear Mary

Thank you for your letter of the 26th. I am very sorry to hear about the earache. It is a horrid thing, much worse than toothache. We all go through periods of dryness in our prayers, don't we? I doubt (but ask your *directeur*) whether they are necessarily a bad symptom. I sometimes suspect that what we *feel* to be our best prayers are really our worst; that what we are enjoying is the satisfaction of apparent success, as in executing a dance or reciting a poem. Do our prayers sometimes go wrong because we insist on trying to talk to God when He wants to talk to us. Joy tells me that once, years ago, she was haunted one morning by a feeling that God wanted something of her, a persistent pressure like the nag of a neglected duty. And till mid-morning she kept on wondering what it was. But the moment she stopped worrying, the answer came through as plain as a spoken voice. It was "I don't want you to *do* anything. I want to *give* you something"; and immediately her heart was full of peace and delight. St. Augustine says "God gives where He finds empty hands". A man whose hands are full of parcels can't receive a gift. Perhaps these parcels are not always sins or earthly cares, but sometimes our own fussy attempts to worship Him in *our* way. Incidentally, what most often interrupts my own prayers is not great distractions but tiny ones— things one will have to do or avoid in the course of the next hour.

We are all well, but tired of the refusal of spring to arrive. I've never known a colder, wetter, darker March. This is pretty early in the morning and Joy is

still asleep: otherwise she would join me in our love
to you.

Yours
Jack

The Kilns,
Headington Quarry,
Oxford
15/4/58

Dear Mary

What lovely news you have to tell. I do thank God
on your behalf most heartily. What strange tricks our
minds play!—that we should think it presumption to
believe what we [are] forbidden *not* to believe.
About past, long past, sins: I had been a Christian for
many years before I *really* believed in the forgiveness
of sins, or more strictly, before my theoretical belief
became a reality to me. I fancy this may not be so
uncommon.

Joy sends her love. We were away at a very nice
country hotel last week having at last, what we never
had before, a honeymoon! Here's another absurdity of
the mind: I'm such a confirmed old bachelor that I
couldn't help feeling I was being rather naughty
("Staying with a woman at a hotel!" Just like people
in the newspapers!) I can't write more, for I'm travelling back to Cambridge to-day and the Vicar is coming in a few minutes to give Joy her Easter Communion (she still can't manage church).

God bless you more and more.

Yours
Jack

P.S.—By the way, you are one of the *minority* of my
numerous female correspondents who didn't gradual-
ly fade away as soon as they heard I was married!

Dear Mary

Perhaps you won't mind a letter from me this time, instead of Jack? He is having his first go at examining for the Cambridge tripos, and is fairly drowning in examination papers—apparently very silly ones! He comes up for air now and then, blows a few pathetic bubbles, then submerges again. He can't even get home for the next fortnight; our longest separation since our marriage, and we're both feeling it badly!

I *am* sorry you've been having that nasty time in the hospital. I know only too well what even the nicest hospital is like; how the nurses all vanish at the one moment of the day when you really need them, how the televisions and wirelesses all around make night hideous, how the night nurse wakes you from the first really refreshing sleep you've had in a month, at midnight, to give you your sleeping pill. . . . And you, I suppose, have been the subject of demonstrations to medical students as well! In Oxford they give students *their* examinations at some poor patient's bedside; examiners and student alike all done up in their mortarboards and gowns, and scaring the patient half to death. But I'm told that experienced patients have been known to whisper the correct diagnosis to the student if he gets stuck. . . .

Well, I hope you're home again now, and that it wasn't too bad and they found the right answers. I can share too in your thwarted desire to be useful. We women feel that more than men, I think. There are a million things that need doing around this house. Once I would have pitched in and helped my housekeeper—but now, because I have to walk with a stick and have only one hand free, I'm more nuisance than help and can only sit on the sidelines and give advice and be a pest. It *is* difficult having to accept all the time! But unless we did, how could the others have the pleasure, and the spiritual growth, of giving? And—I don't know about you, but I was very proud; I liked the superior feeling of helping others, and for me it is much harder to receive than to give but, I think, much more blessed.

Then, too, it's only since I've been ill and helpless that I've realised just how good people in general are, when they have a chance. So many people have taken trouble over me, and gone out of their way to give me pleasure or help! It's very heartwarming—and humbling, for I remember how cynical I used to be about humanity and feel a salutary shame.

Is your pet a cat or dog? I've found that cats stand these changes and separations pretty well—one of mine, when I was ill, took possession of a new home and mistress and had them completely under his thumb in a week. (If one can speak of a cat's thumb?)

Can you do any sort of work? I've found that making crocheted rugs and tablecloths, or knitting socks, was an amazing help with my spiritual difficulties when I was feeling low. One can work off so many frustrations by stabbing away with a knitting needle! It's better to make pretty things, I find, than just useful ones.

Of course we're both praying for you—and don't be too afraid, even if you turn out to need an operation. I've had three, and they were nothing like so bad as my fears.

> Blessings,
> Yours,
> Joy Lewis

Dear Mary

(1.) Remember what St. John says "If our *heart* condemn us, God is stronger than our heart". The *feeling* of being, or not being, forgiven and loved, is not what matters. One must come down to brass tacks. If there is a particular sin on your conscience, repent and confess it. If there isn't, tell the despondent devil not to be silly. You can't help *hearing* his voice (the odious inner radio) but you must treat it merely like a buzzing in your ears or any other irrational nuisance. (2.) Remember the story in the *Imitation,* how the Christ on the crucifix suddenly spoke to the monk who was so anxious about his salvation and said "If you knew that all was well, what would you, to-day, do, or stop doing?" When you have found the answer, do it or stop doing it. You see, one must always get back to the practical and definite. What the devil loves is that vague cloud of unspecified guilt feeling or unspecified virtue by which he lures us into despair or presumption. "Details, please?" is the answer. (3.) The sense of dereliction cannot be a bad symptom for Our Lord Himself experienced it in its depth—"Why hast thou forsaken me?"

Of course we will continue to pray for you.

A *tripos* at Cambridge is an examination: so called for the *tripos* (compare *tripod*) or 3-legged stool on which the candidate used to sit when the exam. was still, not written work, but a disputation.

Joy and I have just been for a lovely fortnight in Ireland. She, and my brother, are both well. We send our loves and blessings.

Yours
Jack

77

Dear Mary

Thanks for your letter of 26th. The *Time* review was ill-timed, for the American edition of the book[1] will not be published until November. I have told Harcourt Brace to send you a copy when it appears. I also have been in the hands of the dentist but much less unpleasantly than you; I know a "dry socket" after an extraction can be the very devil and all. We must both, I'm afraid, recognise that, as we grow older, we become like old cars—more and more repairs and replacements are necessary. We must just look forward to the fine new machines (latest Resurrection model) which are waiting for us, we hope, in the Divine garage! Thank you for the enclosure; I don't think it contradicts anything I've said. Joy continues well, thank God, and would send her love if she were awake, which at the moment she's not, for I'm a barbarously early riser and have usually got my breakfast and dealt with my letters before the rest of the house is astir. One result is that I often enjoy the only fine hours of the day—at this time of the year lovely, still, cool sunshine from 7 till 10, followed by rain from then on, is common. I love the empty, silent, dewy, cobwebby hours. I hope your mouth is now comfortable again.

Yours
Jack

There is an old Scots version of Psalm 136 (137) 8ff which goes:

O blessed may that trooper be

---

[1] Doubtless a reference to *Reflections on the Psalms*.

> Who, riding on his naggie,
> Wull tak thy wee bairns by the taes
> And ding them on the craggie

                                    Magdalene College,
                                          Cambridge.
                                       Oct. 30, 1958

Dear Mary

That is very good news about your daughter and family. Also these last minute mercies which keep on turning up in your financial crises. I suppose living from day to day ("take no thought for the morrow") is precisely what we have to learn—though the Old Adam in me sometimes murmurs that if God wanted me to live like the lilies of the field, I wonder He didn't give me the same lack of nerves and imagination as they enjoy! Or is that just the point, the precise purpose of this Divine paradox and audacity called Man—to do *with* a mind what other organisms do without it? As for wrinkles—pshaw! Why shouldn't we have wrinkles? Honorable insignia of long service in this warfare. All well with us, in haste, with love.

                                    Yours
                                    Jack

                                          The Kilns
                                    Headington Quarry,
                                             Oxford
                                       Dec 25th 1958

Dear Mary

I have let our correspondence get rather disgracefully behind on my side, not from ceasing to think of you, but from being very busy finishing a book[1] (a dull, academic, technical one, tho' exciting to me) and from the usual daily post—drat it! Thanks for

[1] Probably *Studies in Words.*

79

your nice review. And I am glad our law now allows me to send you a little (I gather you and Barfield[2] have it all in train). We are all well—Joy wonderful—but live in perpetual sunlessness. Never knew so long a spell of fogs. One pines for lights and, scarcely less, *shadows,* which make up so much of the beauty of the world. Accept the warmest love and Christmas greetings from us both.

Yours
Jack

The Kilns,
Headington Quarry,
Oxford
Dec 29/58

Dear Mary

Just a very hurried line—(1). To condole with you on the loss of Fr.——.[1] (2.) To tell a story which puts the contrast between *our* feast of the Nativity and, all this ghastly "Xmas" racket at its lowest. My brother heard a woman on a 'bus say, as the 'bus passed a church with a Crib outside it, "Oh Lor'! They bring religion into everything. Look—they're dragging it even into Christmas now!"

Love and sympathy from us both.

Yours
Jack

As from Magdalene
Jan 26th 59

Dear Mary

Thanks for letter of the 26th. Your Grant Ulysses Smith sounds delightful. Did you know that when

---

[1] He was leaving for a year in Palestine.
[2] Owen Barfield, solicitor and lifetime friend of Lewis.

your army was here in the last war your coloured troops were more popular than the white ones? A letter from Cuba with no mention of the revolution is rather surprising at first sight. But it might not even be due to caution. I am often struck in reading the records of the past (e.g. letters written during *our* Civil War in the 17th Century) how unimportant the things the historians make so much of seem to have been to ordinary people who were alive at the time. Does not what we call "history" in fact leave out nearly the whole of real life? Of course the cure mentioned in my article on prayer was Joy: the "good man" an old pupil of mine—one of the completest and most beautiful conversions I have witnessed. By the way, I mentioned to a distinguished theologian that I had been attacked by "a man called N.", and he replied "Oh! old P.N.! What does he believe *this week*?"—so apparently he changes his views pretty often. Perhaps one day he may give Christianity a trial. I have put him in my prayers. I am sorry to hear about the teeth: always a horrid business. We are having beautiful winter weather at present: bright, pale sunshine (paler than you ever see—Joy calls it the "arctic light"), still air, and just that sprinkling of hoar-frost which makes everything sparkle like sugar. All well. Good wishes.

Yours
Jack

Magdalene College,
Cambridge
6/5/59

Dear Mary

I am sorry you have been worried. Actually I was quite unaware that we owed you a letter. But never assume that anything is wrong if I should make the same mistake again. Remember, I don't type. Also, manlike, I am not naturally a correspondent at all. The daily letter-writing I have to do is very laborious to me.

We are all well. Indeed Joy and I both *dig*—a thing neither of us expected ever to do again.

We also have a Siamese cat. In my heart of hearts I really prefer the great, grey bullet-headed native cat, but the Siamese are delicate and fascinating creatures. Ours adores me because I lift her up by her tail—an operation which I can't imagine I should like if I were a cat, but she comes back for more and more, purring all the time.

The young priest after whose laying-on-of hands Joy began so miraculously to mend now writes to tell me that his own wife is suffering from cancer. His name is Peter. Will you, of your charity, have him in your prayers?

Joy, if she were here, would join me in all greetings and good wishes.

Yours
Jack

The Kilns,
Headington Quarry,
Oxford
May 19th 1959

Dear Mary

I am sorry to hear you have lost an old friend. Curiously enough the same thing has just happened to my brother and me—old lady (at least I suppose she must have been old, tho' she was always a girl to us) whom we have known since before we can remember. And, just like you, we keep on hearing jokes for which she would have been exactly *the* right recipient. There is no way out of it: either one must die fairly young or else outlive many friends. We are now told by the learned that Siamese are not royal cats at all, but the common jungle cat of those parts and quite "without honour" in their own country! Another disillusion!

In haste—all blessings.

Yours
Jack

The Kilns
Headington Quarry,
Oxford
June 7th 1959

Dear Mary

I am sorry to hear that so many troubles crowd upon you but glad to hear that, by God's grace, you are so untroubled. So often, whether for good or ill, one's inner state seems to have so little connection with the circumstances. I can *now* hardly bear to look back on the summer before last when Joy was apparently dying and I was often screaming with the pain of osteoporosis; yet at the time we were in reality far from unhappy. May the peace of God continue to infold you. Your elderly neighbour would be comic if the matters at issue were not so serious. She has an odd idea of how to cheer people up! Like having a visit from a ghoul. People in real life are often so preposterous that one would not dare to put them in a novel. I gather you are having a heat-wave in America, and I hope this won't make things harder for you. We have had a lot of (for us) hot weather; now, though the heat has gone, the drought continues and the soil in our garden is like dust.

What a state we have got into when we can't say "I'll be happy when God calls me" without being afraid one will be thought "morbid". After all, St. Paul said just the same. If we really believe what we say we believe—if we really think that home is elsewhere and that this life is a "wandering to find home", why should we not look forward to the arrival. There are, aren't there, only three things we can do about death: to desire it, to fear it, or to ignore it. The third alternative, which is the one the modern world calls "healthy" is surely the most uneasy and precarious of all. We are well here. God bless you.

Yours
Jack

The Old Inn
Crawfordsburn
Co. Down,
Northern Ireland
July 7th 1959

Dear Mary

Your letter of the 20th has followed us here. You seem to have had a very nasty experience. I can see why you describe it as "looking into the face of death"; but who knows whether that face, when we really look at it, will be at all like that? Let us hope better things. I had a tooth out the other day, and came away wondering whether we dare hope that the moment of death may be very like that delicious moment when one realises that the tooth is really out and a voice says "Rinse your mouth out with this". "This" of course will be Purgatory.

What you have gone through begins to reconcile me to our Welfare State of which I have said so many hard things. "National Health Service" with free treatment for all has its drawbacks—one being that Doctors are incessantly pestered by people who have nothing wrong with them. But it is better than leaving people to sink or swim on their own resources.

You surely don't mean "feeling that we are not *worthy* to be forgiven"? For of course we aren't. Forgiveness by its nature is for the unworthy. You mean "Feeling that we *are not* forgiven." I have known that. I "believed" theoretically in the divine forgiveness for years before it really came home to me. It is a wonderful moment when it does.

I am sorry this is so illegible but we are away on holiday and I have only Joy's biro[1] to write with. Odious thing! We have been having a nice time, tho' not very good weather. Love and sympathy from both.

Yours
Jack

The Kilns,
Headington Quarry,
Oxford
11 July 1959

Dear Mary

We got back from Ireland last night, when I found an infinite pile of letters awaiting me, so this can be only a hurried scrawl. Your doctor sounds delightful and I am glad you have that comfort. Not that I know what a *pediatrician* is any more than a boojum! All our good wishes go with you.

Yours
Jack

The Kilns etc
Aug 3/59

Dear Mary

I have your letter of 30 July. It has puzzled me. I understood that you were going to the doctors for heart trouble. How and why do the psychiatrists come

[1] A ball-point pen.

into the picture? But since they have come, I am glad to hear they are nice. I sympathise most deeply with you on the loss of your friend. But for good as well as for ill one never knows what is coming next. You remember the *Imitation* says "Bear your cross, for if you try to get rid of it you will probably find another and worse one". But there is a brighter side to the same principle. When we lose one blessing, another is often most unexpectedly given in its place. We are all well here though I am frantically busy; and though I get no more tired now than I did when I was younger, I take much longer to get un-tired afterwards. All blessings and sympathy.

Yours
Jack

The Kilns,
Headington Quarry,
Oxford
21 Aug 59

Dear Mary

Yes, six snacks instead of three meals must be a frightful nuisance. One must be always washing up! And I know how, when one is on one's own, even a nice meal and a good appetite can hardly make the whole time-wasting business getting it and clearing it away seem worth the few minutes of actual eating. You will be surprised to hear that our temperatures are, for once, not very much lower than yours. Yesterday at 11.30 a.m. on our lawn the thermometer read 94 degrees. A big tree and a still bigger branch off another came crashing down in the wood yesterday, in windless calm—purely for lack of internal moisture. The early mornings and late evenings are lovely, but not the blistering hours in between.

A "move" is a beastly thing at the best of times.

One's things have a sort of whining pathos (do you know what I mean) about them once they are winkled out of their old native haunts.

I wish you had better news to send me and I more comfort to send you. Of course you are always in my prayers.

The house is still asleep—I get up early and try to dispose of my mail in the day's cool and silent hours, so I can send you only *my* love and sympathy. Joy would add hers if she were awake!

Yours
Jack

The Kilns etc
21 Sept [1959]

Dear Mary

In great haste—indeed no more than a scrape of the pen to express my sympathy. House-hunting is gruelling and heart-breaking work at the best of times. I'm sorry I missed Fr. L. How pleased you must be about selling that article! Ah well here. If *I* got a crocodile skin I'd sell it! Blessings.

Yours
Jack

The Kilns,
Headington Quarry,
Oxford
18 Oct 59

Dear Mary

Well, thank goodness your move is now over. A "bed-sitter", as we call them over here, has certainly its drawbacks. In England, where most houses have no central heating, it has one compensation—that of going to bed and getting up in a warm room. But that, I suppose, would be so anyway in America. . . .

Will you redouble your prayers for us? Apparently the wonderful recovery Joy made in 1957 was only a reprieve, not a pardon. The last x-ray check reveals cancerous spots returning in many of her bones. There seems to be some hope of a few years life still and there are still things the doctors can do. But they are all in the nature of "rearguard actions". We are in retreat. The tide has turned. Of course God can do again what He did before. The sky is not now so dark as it was when I married her in hospital. Her courage is wonderful and she gives me more support than I can give her.

The dreadful thing, as you know, is the waking each morning—the moment at which it all flows back on one.

Yours
Jack

The Kilns,
Headington Quarry,
Oxford
22 Dec 1959

Dear Mary

I have got your note. It finds me with as clear a conscience about correspondence as a not very methodical, nor leisured, man ever has. I am pretty sure I have written to you since I last heard from you. Let us, however, make a compact that, if we are both alive next year, whenever we write to one another it shall *not* be at Christmas time. That period is becoming a sort of nightmare to me—it means endless quilldriving!

Despite the terrible news of which I told you, we hobble along wonderfully well. I am ashamed (yet in a way pleased) to tell you that it is Joy who supports

me rather than I her. I do not forget your prayers
and am most grateful for them.

I hope you are now fully settled into your new
quarters and find them tolerable! Also that "Brother
Ass"[1] is behaving better.

Christmas will be over by the time you get this, but
you know you will have been (as always) in my
thoughts and prayers. Let us hope that both of us will
have been given Grace, amidst all this ghastly commercial racket of "Xmas", to enter into the feast of the
Nativity: the racket has nearly smothered it!

Yours
Jack

The Kilns,
Headington Quarry,
Oxford
13 Feb. 1960

Dear Mary

I am sorry to hear from your letter of 8 Feb. about
the "Asian flu". Either we haven't yet got it here or
our doctors call it by some other name. I very much
hope that by the time this reaches you, you will be
really on the mend. Many thanks for the pretty card
and poem you sent Joy—it was a kind thought. She
remains so far amazingly well and strong to all ap-
pearances, thank God. It looks as if we shall after all
be able to manage a lightning air-trip to Greece
which was arranged in happier times. It would mean
a great deal to both of us to have stood even once on
the Acropolis. I am suffering from a strange condition
which makes it impossible ever to *stay* asleep (I can
go to sleep easily enough) for more than about 70
min. continuously at night, or to *stay* awake in the

---

[1] St. Francis' expression for the *body*.

day time if I relax at all! Premature senility perhaps.
God keep us all,

Yours
Jack

The Kilns,
Headington Quarry,
Oxford
26 March 1960

Dear Mary

Do you know, I should have more hope for the young cad described in Fr. L's letter than for many people in a quiet, cultured state of unbelief who would always speak of Christianity with reverence? His very rudeness shows that he is not quite free from the fear that there "might be something in it after all". I bet that if he were talking to Hindoos or Buddhists he would speak more politely of *their* religion. You must be having the same flu' bug that has visited us. His visits are not always very severe, but it is a wonderful *stayer*.

Things are not, or not much, worse with us, but life is very terrible. I sometimes feel I am mad to be taking Joy to Greece in her present condition, but her heart is set upon it. They give the condemned man what he likes for his last breakfast, I am told.

I hope *your* news will soon be better,

Yours
Jack

As from Magdalene,
Cambridge
19/4/60

Dear Mary

We did get to Greece, and it was a wonderful success. Joy performed prodigies, climbing to the top of the Acropolis and getting as far as the Lion gate of Mycenae. She has (no wonder) come back very exhausted and full of aches. But I would not have had her denied it. The condemned man is allowed his favourite breakfast even if it is indigestible. She was absolutely enraptured by what she saw. But pray for us: the sky grows very dark.

I can't begin to describe Greece. Attica is hauntingly beautiful and Rhodes is an earthly paradise—all orange and lemon orchards and wild flowers and vines and olives, and the mountains of Asia on the horizon. And lovely, cheap wines. I've eaten squid and octopus!

Yours
Jack

The Kilns,
Headington Quarry,
Oxford
15 July 1960

Dear Mary

I've just got your letter of the 12th. Joy died on the 13th. I can't describe the apparent unreality of my life since then. She received absolution and died at peace with God. I will try to write again when I have more command of myself. I'm like a sleep-walker at the moment. God bless.

Yours
Jack

The Kilns,
Headington Quarry,
Oxford
24 Sept. 1960

Dear Mary

Thanks for your letter of the 21st. I hope from what

you say that the end of this bad patch is now in sight. Meantime, you seem in fine spiritual health.

As to *how* I take sorrow, the answer is "In nearly all the possible ways". Because, as you probably know, it isn't a state but a process. It keeps on changing—like a winding road with quite a new landscape at each bend. Two curious discoveries I have made. The moments at which you call most desperately and clamorously to God for help are precisely those when you seem to get none. And the moments at which I feel nearest to Joy are precisely those when I mourn her *least*. Very queer. In both cases a clamorous need seems to shut one off from the thing needed. No one ever told me this. It is almost like "Don't knock and it shall be opened to you". I must think it over.

My younger stepson is the greatest comfort to me. My brother is still away in Ireland.

God bless us all.

> Yours
> Jack

> Magdalene College,
> Cambridge
> 28 Oct. 1960

Dear Mary

Dear, dear, this is very distressing news. How many things have come upon you at once! As Coleridge says

—to be wroth with one we love

Doth work like madness in the brain.

It's the mixture, or alternation, of resentment and affection that is so very uneasy, isn't it? For the indulgence of either immediately comes slap up against the other, which then, a few seconds later comes slap up against it, so that the mind does a diabolical "shuttle-service" to and fro between them. We've all at some time in our lives, I expect, had this experience. Except possibly anxiety nothing is more hostile to sleep. One must try, I suppose, to keep on remembering that the love part of the suffering is good and purgatorial while the anger part is bad and infernal. Yet how madly one cherishes that base part as if it were one's dearest possession—dwells on everything that can aggravate the offence—and keep on thinking of things one would like to say to the other party! I suppose all one can do is to keep on meditating on the petition "Forgive us our trespasses *as we* forgive those that trespass against *us*". I find *Fear* a great help—the fear that my own unforgivingness will exclude me from all the promises. Fear tames wrath. And *this* fear (we have Our Lord's word for it) is wholly well-grounded. The human heart (mine anyway) is "desperately wicked". Joy often quoted this in connection with the great difficulty she found in forgiving a very near and very nasty relative of her own. One has to keep on doing it over again, doesn't one?

God send you help of every sort.

Yours
Jack

P.S.—It's also useful to think "Either X is not so bad as, in my present anger, I think. If not, how unjust I must be. If so, how terribly X needs my prayers".

Magdalene College,
Cambridge
24 Nov 1960

Dear Mary

Thanks for your letter of the 20th. About forgetting things. Dr. Johnson said "If, on leaving the company, a young man cannot remember where he has left his hat, it is nothing. But when an old man forgets, everyone says, Ah, his memory is going". So with ourselves. We have *always* been forgetting things: but now, when we do so, we attribute it to our age. Why, it was years ago that, on finishing my work before lunch, I stopped myself only just in time from putting my cigarette-end into my spectacle case and throwing my spectacles into the fire!

What I was writing about last time was the pain and resentment you were feeling about some things ——had said or done. I wasn't trying to lecture. Rather, to compare notes about temptation we all have to contend with.

There, by the way, is a sentence ending with a preposition. The silly "rule" against it was invented by Dryden. I think he disliked it only because you can't do it in either French or Latin which he thought more "polite" languages than English.

As for the bug-bear of Old Peoples' Homes, remember that our ignorance works both ways. Just as some of the things we have longed and hoped for turn out to be dust and ashes when we get them, so the things we have most dreaded sometimes turn out to be quite nice. If you ever do have to go to a Home, Christ will be there just as much as in any other place.

The bit of conversation with——which you quoted sounds as if there were nothing much wrong on either side but nerves. But I admit I don't know the cure. Slowing down the *speed* of the conversation (so far as this depends on oneself) is sometimes helpful. Also sitting down. I think we all talk more excitedly when standing (Notice how often the actors in a comedy *sit* whereas those in a tragedy usually stand).

All blessings,
Yours
Jack

Dear Mary

I don't feel at all "wise" and the only bit of advice I can give you with perfect confidence is—*don't* sit up writing long letters either to me or to anyone else when you are tired! It is very bad for you. Now as to the main issue.

Whatever you decide to *do*, get your own attitude right. . . .

Their penitence may no doubt be very imperfect and their motives very mixed. But so are all *our* repentances and all *our* motives. Accept theirs as you hope God will accept yours. Remember that He has promised to forgive you *as*, and only *as*, you forgive them.

The decision, however, remains, I agree, a terrible one to make, and only someone who really knew you ... is really qualified to give you advice. ... Of course this would involve giving up a great deal. ... But I'm afraid as we grow older life consists more and more in either giving up things or waiting for them to be taken from us. . . .

The only certain thing is that your acceptance (if you accept) or your refusal (if you refuse) must be made with perfect charity and courtesy. May God's grace give you the necessary humility. Try not to think—much less, speak—of *their* sins. One's own are a much more profitable theme! And if, on consideration, one can find no faults on one's own side, then cry for mercy: for this *must* be a most dangerous delusion. . . .

Well, I'm afraid all this comes to precious little. But I don't, and can't *know* enough. I can only pray that you may be guided to the right choice. It is (no disguising it) only a choice between Crosses. The more one can accept that fact, the less one can think about happiness on earth, the less, I believe, one suffers. Or at any rate the suffering becomes more purgatorial and less infernal.

Yours
Jack

Magdalene College,
Cambridge.
24 Feb. 1961

Dear Mary

I am very glad you have made the decision and I believe it is the right one. . . . There will be every opportunity and necessity of mortifying the "highly developed pride" diagnosed by the grapho-analyst! There will have to be plenty of "turning back" and "change of purpose"—except, to be sure, the constant and prayerful purpose of continual sacrifice. The great thing is that you realise all that, and as the comic beatitude says "Blessed are they that expect little for they shall not be disappointed". . . . Probably the safe rule will be "When in doubt what to do or say, do or say nothing". I feel this very much with my stepsons. I so easily *meddle* and *gas*: when all the time what will really influence them, for good or ill, is not anything I do or say but what I *am*. And this unfortunately one can't know and can't much alter, though God can. Two rules from Wm. Law must be always before our minds.

1. "There can be no surer proof of a confirmed pride than a belief that one is sufficiently humble".

2. "I earnestly beseech all who conceive they have

suffered an affront to believe that it is very much less than they suppose".

I hope your vet is not a charlatan? Psychological diagnoses even about human patients seem to me pretty phoney. They must be even phonier when applied to animals. You can't put a cat on a couch and make it tell you its dreams or produce words by "free association". Also—I have a great respect for cats—they are very shrewd people and would probably see through the analyst a good deal better than he'd see through them.

Remember me kindly to Fr. D'Arcy.

Jobs bunch oddly in my profession and for the last fortnight I have been so busy as hardly to know whether I'm on my head or my heels and am very tired. Otherwise well enough. We keep on having spring and winter alternately, and however few or many blankets one starts the night with one will wake up either sweating or shivering before morning. . . . You will all be much in my prayers.

Yours
Jack

The Kilns,
Headington Quarry,
Oxford
28 March 1961

Dear Mary

Humans are very seldom either totally sincere or totally hypocritical. Their moods change, their motives are mixed, and they are often themselves quite mistaken as to what their motives are. . . .

I know it's easy for me to give good advice to others in situations which I probably could not face myself. But that can't be helped; I must say what I think true. Surely the main purpose of our life is to reach the point at which "one's own life as a person" *is* at an end. One must in this sense "die", become "naught", relinquish one's freedom and independence. "Not I, but Christ that dwelleth in me"— "He must grow greater and I must grow less"—"He that loseth his life shall find it". But you know all this quite as well as I do. It may well involve eating white bread instead of brown! How many millions at this moment have no bread at all. All blessings.

Yours
Jack

P.S.—Of course this little addition to your income can continue.[1]

Magdalene College,
Cambridge.
21 April 1961

Dear Mary

I have your letter of the 16th. . . . Thanks for the poem. I've got some sort of virus into me which has kept me from being quite well all this spring, never quite awake by day and never quite asleep by night (and never without unpleasant dreams), so don't expect much from me. Blessings on you all.

Yours
Jack

Magdalene College,
Cambridge
5 June 1961

Dear Mary

. . I have nothing to say but things you know already quite as well as I do. We must beware of the

---

[1] For some time Lewis had been having his American publisher send her a small monthly stipend.

Past, mustn't we? I mean that any fixing of the mind on old evils beyond what is absolutely necessary for repenting our own sins and forgiving those of others is certainly useless and usually bad for us. Notice in Dante that the lost souls are entirely concerned with their past! Not so the saved. This is one of the dangers of being, like you and me, old. There's so much past, now, isn't there? And so little else. But we must try very hard not to keep on endlessly chewing the cud. We must look forward more eagerly to sloughing that old skin off forever—metaphors getting a bit mixed here, but you know what I mean.

I almost dare to believe my digestion is coming right again, but I am so tired out with it and with marking exam papers that there isn't much left of me at the moment! God bless us all.

Yours
Jack

The Kilns, Kiln Lane,
Headington Quarry,
Oxford.
12th July 1961.

Dear Mrs. ————

I've opened your letter of 6th addressed to my brother, who is, I'm sorry to say at present in hospital and unable to deal with his own mail. I saw him yesterday and mentioned that a letter had arrived from you, and he asked me to explain why there will be no answer to it for quite a time.

With kind regards.

Yours sincerely,
W. H. Lewis

The Kilns, Kiln Lane,
Headington Quarry,
Oxford.
20th August 1961.

Dear Mrs. ─────

Many thanks for yours of the 14th, which I answer
because you ask me to do so. This sounds a little
ungracious, but what I mean is that I really have no
news to give you. What there is, is good though,
thank God. The kidney condition which has been
holding everything up is improving rapidly and the
doctor is very satisfied with him. His last blood test
was excellent. He is, so far as a sick man can be, in the
best of spirits, eating well, hungry and what we all
take to be a splendid sign, is beginning to complain
of being *bored*—which is very different from even a
fortnight ago when he was quite content to doze
away each day.

On his and my own behalf I send you grateful
thanks for your prayers.

Yours sincerely,
W. H. Lewis

The Kilns, Kiln Lane,
Headington Quarry,
Oxford.
7th October 1961.

Dear Mrs. ─────

I have your letter of the 5th addressed to Jack, but
I'm sure you will understand why you are not getting
a personal reply to it. Not that he isn't really making
a recovery, but the process is very slow, he does get
so tired, and so easily, and consequently we don't
give him any of his letters to answer unless they are
on quite unavoidable business. But he is grateful for
yours, and for your kind anxiety.

The position at the moment is this. Jack has had a series of blood transfusions in hospital and the result was that he came home a week ago most definitely improved; with not only the permission but the encouragement of his doctors, he now gets up in the morning and cooks his own breakfast, and every day he goes out for half an hour's walk. Better still, he has been put on a more generous diet and enjoys his meals. But perhaps the best sign is that he tells me he is getting very bored with invalid life and is itching to get back to work. As for the impending operation, the surgeon now talks of it as a thing quite in the future—six, or even twelve months ahead he says. Which naturally is an enormous relief to me, for if they are taking this view there cannot be anything very urgent the matter. In fact on the whole I'm a much happier man than I was when I last wrote to you. With kindest regards,

Yours sincerely,
W. H. Lewis

The Kilns
Headington Quarry
Oxford
23 Dec 1961

Dear Mary

We both seem to be having a sticky time at present? I am much the same; that is, I keep on looking and feeling better but each new blood count shows that I have made no real progress.

I've been greatly impressed by the work of an American Trappist called Thomas Merton—*No Man Is An Island*. You probably know it?

I can't write much at present. All blessings.

Yours
Jack

The Kilns,
Headington Quarry,
Oxford
17 Jan 62

Dear Mary

I am distressed by all you tell me. Alas! advances in hygiene have made most of us live longer but other things have made old age harsher than it ever was before. It is a pity that the old usually dislike *one* another. In your position I myself would prefer a "Home"—or almost anything—to solitude. Your view reminds me of a dipsomaniac retired major I once knew who refused the suggestion that he should try A.A. on the ground that "it would be full of retired majors"! I am better, but that only means more nearly ripe for a big operation. I still can't write much. With deepest sympathy,

Yours
Jack

The Kilns.
6 April 62

Dear Mary

My news is neither good nor bad. On the one hand they have decided that my kidneys will never be fit for the operation: on the other, that I have developed a tolerance for my present condition and can carry on indefinitely in a semi-invalid way without surgery. I am sorry to hear you have run into more trouble.

Yours
Jack

Magdalene College,
Cambridge
4 May 62

Dear Mary

Thank you all for your kind prayers. You have mine daily. Yes—it is sometimes hard to obey St. Paul's "Rejoice". We must try to take life moment by moment. The actual *present* is usually pretty tolerable, I think, if only we refrain from adding to its burden that of the past and the future. How right Our Lord is about "sufficient to the day". Do even pious people in their reverence for the more radiantly divine element in His sayings, sometimes attend too little to their sheer practical common-sense? I was charmed with your two Chinese children. It reminded me of an adventure Joy and I had in Crete, when Joy gave a few drachmae to a very starved looking little girl (She wasn't begging—just looking at us with a child's open-eyed curiosity). The girl instantly rushed into a neighbouring thicket and returned with her hands full of fruit for us. (It was a nice fruit which we'd never seen before, but all our efforts to find out its name elicited only the word *karpos*, which simply means "fruit"!).

Yours
Jack

Magdalene College,
Cambridge
Ascension Day 1962

Dear Mary

Yes. The doctors allowed me to come back to work this term "experimentally". So far the experiment has been a great success. I am better than I have ever been since last June. But I am permanently a semi-invalid on a low-protein diet (it must be good for my soul when there are things I really like for dinner and I mustn't have them!). Like you, I have to reduce stair-climbing to the minimum. It does make life *complicated*, doesn't it? There's no going back upstairs for something you have forgotten, so that every time one goes down one has to think of everything as if one were planning an expedition to the North Pole or central Africa. But one learns!

All you tell me about China is horrible, and I was shocked to read an article the other day about Portugal. I had got the idea that Salazar was (as if such a thing were possible!) a *good* dictator. But apparently Portugal is just like all the other totalitarian countries, indeed worse in one way, for the atrocities are done in the name of Christianity. As a verse in our version of the Psalter says "All the earth is full of darkness and cruel habitations".

I'm sorry my letters are so short compared with yours, but I'm afraid this is an irremovable difference between the sexes—women love letter writing and men loathe it. And there is so much *other* writing in my day's work!

Something has gone wrong with spring this year and we are still having winter weather. The cuckoo *has* arrived, very late. But I bet he wishes he'd stayed in sunnier climes.

Yours
Jack

The Kilns,
Headington Quarry,
Oxford
3/7/62

Dear Mary

Yes, we do seem to be having a certain amount of experience in common! Perhaps if we had done more

104

voluntary fasting before God would not now have put us on these darn diets! Well, the theologians say that an imposed mortification can have all the merit of a voluntary one if it is taken in the right spirit. We are also both ruled by cats. Joy's Siamese—my "stepcat" as I call her—is the most terribly conversational animal I ever knew. She talks all the time and wants doors and windows to be opened for her 1000 times an hour. Yes, and one gets bored with the medicines too—besides always wondering "Did I remember to take them after breakfast?" and then wondering whether the risk of missing a dose or the risk of an over dose is the worst! All my sympathy. In haste.

Yours
Jack

Magdalene College,
Cambridge
31/7/62

Dear Mary

Yes, it *is* strange that anyone should dislike cats. But cats themselves are the worst offenders in this respect. They very seldom seem to like one another.

I have a notion that, apart from actual pain, men and women are quite diversely afflicted by illness. To a woman one of the great evils about it is that she can't do things. To a man (or anyway a man like me) the great consolation is the reflection "Well, anyway, no one can now demand that I should *do* anything". I have often had the fancy that one stage in Purgatory might be a great big kitchen in which things are always going wrong—milk boiling over, crockery getting smashed, toast burning, animals stealing. The women have to learn to sit still and mind their own business: the men have to learn to jump up and do something about it. When both sexes have mastered this exercise, they go on to the next....

I think I continue to improve physically. As I get better I feel the loss of Joy more. I suppose the capacity for happiness must re-awake before one becomes fully aware of its absence.

Yes, one gets sick of pills. But thank God we don't live in the age of horrible medicines such as our grandparents had to swallow.

All blessings.

Yours
Jack

The Kilns,
Headington Quarry,
Oxford
3 Sept 62

Dear Mary

Our situations are curiously reversed: you live in fear that an operation may be necessary, and I in hope that one may become possible. (At least it ought to be *hope*, but sometimes the flesh is weak!). Nausea is horrible, isn't it? Worse than all but really severe pains: at least it dominates the mind and the emotions more.

I am surprised that you should doubt your forgiveness for sins from which you have doubtless long since received absolution. Especially as what apparently troubles you is not malice but the unforeseen results (or things only possibly the result) of behaviour whose intention was innocent. No doubt, as I know only too well, the knowledge that one's acts have, contrary to one's intention, led to all sorts of dreadful consequences, is a heavy burden. But it is a burden of regret and humiliation, isn't it?, rather than of guilt. Perhaps we all dislike humiliation so much that we tend to disguise it from ourselves by treating blunders as sins? . . .

Of course you always have my prayers.

My idea of the Purgatorial kitchen didn't mean that anyone had lately been "getting in my hair". It is simply my lifelong experience—that men are more likely to hand over to others what they ought to do themselves, and women more likely to do themselves what others wish they would leave alone. Hence both sexes must be told "Mind your own business", but in two different senses!

Yours

Jack

P.S. There is no question at all of my going to America at present.

The Kilns,
Headington Quarry,
Oxford
2 Oct. 62

Dear Mary

What a horrible treatment! One easily gets to dread the doctors more than the diseases. And I can sympathise with you about old Mrs.——. I saw a great deal of a woman like that at one time. *One* trouble about habitual liars is that, since you can't believe anything they say, you can't feel the slightest interest in it. One has to keep on saying "But for the Grace of God, there go I". Let us pray that we never become like that. . . .

"I am glad to hear you have rehabilitated a displaced cat. I can't understand the people who say cats are not affectionate. Our Siamese (my "stepcat") is almost suffocatingly so. True, our ginger Tom (a great Don Juan and a mighty hunter before the Lord) will take no notice of *me*, but he will of others.

He thinks I'm not quite socially up to his standards, and makes this very clear. No creature can give such a crushing "snub" as a cat! He sometimes looks at the dog—a big Boxer puppy, very anxious to be friendly—in a way that makes it want to sink into the floor.

I never could find out what the VIIth Day Adventists believe, tho' I had a long talk with one the other day, a professor of electrical engineering from your country. I fear it is very mixed up with attempts to interpret the prophecies in the Book of Daniel—not, to my mind, a very profitable undertaking. But he was a grand young chap, sweet as a nut and absolutely sincere. No fool, either.

Prayers as usual!

Yours
Jack

Magdalene College,
Cambridge
26 Oct 62

Dear Mary

I do most thoroughly agree with your father's principle about alms. It will not bother me in the hour of death to reflect that I have been "had for a sucker" by any number of impostors; but it would be a torment to know that one had refused even *one* person in need. After all, the parable of the sheep and goats makes our duty perfectly plain, doesn't it. Another thing that annoys me is when people say "Why did you give that man money? He'll probably go and drink it". My reply is "But if I'd kept [it] *I* should probably have drunk it". The old negro sounds delightful. Is the Catholic University Encyclopedia the same as the "New Catholic Encyclopedia" to which I was lately asked to contribute the article on Medieval Romance? (I didn't; more work than I can manage now). I am sorry to hear of the little dog's death. The animal creation is a strange mystery. We can make some attempt to understand human suffering: but the sufferings of animals from the beginning of the world till now (inflicted not only by us but by one another)—what is one to think?[1] And again, how strange that God brings us into such intimate relations with creatures of whose real purpose and destiny we remain forever ignorant. We know to some degree what angels and men are *for*. But what is a flea for, or a wild dog? What you say about the VII Day Adventists interests me extremely. If they have so much charity there must be something very right about them. . . .

And what is a "wall can opener"? It suggests either opening a tin by means of a wall or opening a wall by means of a tin, and both sound very strange operations.

Well, now to the other letters. Always, prayers.

Yours
Jack

Magdalene College,
Cambridge
8 Nov 62

Dear Mary

.... I nominally have [a place of my own] and am nominally master of the house, but things seldom go as I would have chosen. The truth is that the only alternatives are either solitude (with all its miseries and dangers, both moral and physical) or else all the rubs and frustrations of a joint life. The second, even at its worst seems to me far the better. I hope one is rewarded for all the stunning replies one thinks of

[1] Cf. the chapter "Animal Pain" in Lewis's *The Problem of Pain*.

one does not utter! But alas, even when we don't *say* them, more than we suspect comes out in our look, our manner, and our voice. An elaborately patient silence can be very provoking! We are *all* fallen creatures and *all* very hard to live with. . . .

I do hope the operation will turn out to be unnecessary.

Yours
Jack

The Kilns
Headington Quarry,
Oxford
26 Nov. 62

Dear Mary

My stuff about animals came long ago in *The Problem of Pain*. I ventured the supposal—it could be nothing more—that as we are raised *in* Christ, so at least some animals are raised *in* us. Who knows, indeed, but that a great deal even of the inanimate creation is raised *in* the redeemed souls who have, during this life, taken its beauty into themselves? That may be the way in which the "new heaven and the new earth" are formed. Of course we can only guess and wonder. But these particular guesses arise in me, I trust, from taking seriously the resurrection of the body: a doctrine which now-a-days is very soft pedalled by nearly all the faithful—to our great impoverishment. Not that you and I have now much reason to rejoice in having bodies! Like old automobiles, aren't they? where all sorts of apparently different things keep going wrong, but what they add up to is the plain fact that the machine is wearing out. Well, it was not meant to last forever. Still, I have a kindly feeling for the old rattle-trap. Through it God showed me that whole side of His beauty which is embodied in colour, sound, smell and size. No doubt it has often led me astray: but not half so often, I suspect, as my soul has led *it* astray. For the spiritual evils which we share with the devils (pride, spite) are far worse than what we share with the beasts: and sensuality really arises more from the imagination than from the appetites; which, if left merely to their own animal strength, and not elaborated by our imagination, would be fairly easily managed. But this is turning into a sermon!

Yours
Jack

The Kilns
Headington Quarry
Oxford
10 Dec 62

Dear Mary

Thanks for your letter and the amusing enclosure. What *is* a Magna Charta badge?—quite a "new one on me". About ancient lineage (I haven't any myself). My feeling is that all such things can legitimately be enjoyed provided one takes them lightly enough. Like tinsel crowns worn for private theatricals! And the prig who considers himself *above* enjoying his tinsel crown is perhaps as far astray as the paranoiac who mistakes it for gold. This goes for things like beauty, talent, fame etc. as well as for blood (Of course a great deal of so-called "democratic" feeling against the claims of blood is really based on a desire to make the claims of money all important; and of all claims to distinction money is, I suppose, the basest).

There is much that is cheering, along with much that isn't, in your letter. One must get over any false shame about accepting necessary help. One never *has* been "independent". Always, in some mode or other, one has lived on others, economically, intellectually, spiritually. Who, after all, is *less* independent than someone with "a private income"—every penny of which has been earned by the skill and labour of others? Poverty merely *reveals* the helpless dependence which has all the time been our real condition. We are members of one another whether we choose to recognise the fact or not.

I get on fairly well. My chief trouble is a difficulty in sleeping at night and keeping awake by day. Perhaps I am turning into a nocturnal animal. Bat? Wolf? Owl? Let's hope it will be owl, the bird of wisdom (And I always *was* attracted by mice!)

Yours
Jack

The Kilns,
Headington Quarry,
Oxford.
2 Jan 63

Dear Mary

. . . . As for looks—do most women value *beauty* in a man at all? My experience is that they rather distrust and dislike it. We are having something more like an American winter than we've had for nearly a century, and as we are not prepared for it (very little central heating, no snowploughs, etc) it hits us very hard. There will be real famine conditions in a week or so if a thaw doesn't come. This, with the ghastly drudgery of Christmas mails—they get heavier every year—has left us in a very chastened and un-festive frame of mind! Let's hope 63 will be a better year for us all!

Yours
Jack

The Kilns
8 Jan '63

Dear Mary

I don't mind betting that the things which "had to be done" in your room didn't really *have* to be done at all. Very few things really do. After one bad night with my heart—not so bad as yours, for it was only suffocation, not pain—my doctor strictly rationed me on stairs, and I have obeyed him. Of course it is hideously inconvenient, but that can be put up with and must. What worse than inconvenience would have resulted if you had left those "things" undone? Do take more care of yourself and less of "things"!

Still snow-bound,

Yours
Jack

The Kilns
26/1/63

Dear Mary

That wedding party would have half killed me! and I am afraid it was very bad for you. I too am having bad nights. I find the best sedative if one is wakeful in the middle of the night is—simply FOOD. Have a few biscuits on the table by your bed. I'd a queer night a week ago. Something (not dangerous but a little painful) went wrong at about 1.30 a.m. and needed the surgeon so rang up for ambulance. But as our drive is impassible to wheeled traffic with the snow drifts I had to go out and wait for said ambulance in the road: from about 2 to 2.20. Nice to *look* at: full moon on snow. But I thought my ears would have dropped off with the cold! Got back to bed about 6 o'clock. Your young friend can get the *P. of Pain* in a paper-back in America. Mails perfectly frightful just now. I suppose the snow keeps people in

doors and that encourages them to write letters! In
haste

>   Yours
>   Jack

>   Magdalene College,
>   Cambridge
>   8 Feb 63

Dear Mary

I'm not surprised at Son Suez's reaction. She
couldn't possibly know that this inexplicable arrest,
exile, and imprisonment had a kind intention. It suggests the comforting thought that the strange and
terrifying things which happen to *us* are really for our
benefit. That's an old platitude of course; but seeing it
the other way round, in relation to the cat, somehow
brings it to life.

Still snow!

>   Yours
>   Jack

>   The Kilns,
>   Headington Quarry,
>   Oxford
>   19 March 63

Dear Mary

I am sorry they threaten you with a painful disease. "Dangerous" matters much less, doesn't it? What
have you and I got to do but make our exit? When
they told me I was in danger several months ago, I
don't remember feeling distressed. I am talking, of
course, about *dying*, not about *being killed*. If shells
started falling about this house I should feel quite
differently. An external, visible, and (still worse) au-
dible threat at once wakes the instinct of self-
preservation into fierce activity. I don't think natural

death has any similar terrors. I am thrilled to hear
that Son Suez has a sweater! Is this part of the
demarché (it's in all our papers) which a body of
American women are making to the President to get
animals properly clothed "in the interests of decen-
cy"? Can it be true? If so, not only what insanity, but
also (as in all super-refinements) what fundamental
foulmindedness! But also, what fun! The elephant
looks as if he wore trousers already, but terribly bag-
gy ones. What he needs is *braces*. The Rhino seems to
wear a suit much too big for him: can it be "taken
in"? What sort of collars will giraffes wear? Will seals
and otters have ordinary clothes or bathing suits? The
hedgehog will wear his shirts out terribly quickly, I
should think. The reason I stood out waiting for the
ambulance was that the 200 yards of avenue which
lead up to this house were under such deep snow-
drifts that wheeled traffic couldn't reach the house.
You get arctic winters much more often than we, but
you have no idea what they are like when they do
fall in a country where no-one is prepared for them.
But it didn't do me the slightest harm. In my experience colds and coughs come from infection far more
often than from exposure. Yes, private communions
(I shared many during Joy's last days) are extraordi-
narily moving. I am in danger of preferring them to
those in church.

Blessings and prayers.

Yours
Jack

The Kilns
22 April 63

Dear Mary

What in Heaven's name is "distressing" about an
old man saying to an old woman that they haven't

much more to do here? I wasn't in the least expressing resentment or despondency. I was referring to an obvious fact and one which I don't find either distressing or embarrassing. Do you?

Didn't the flowers all say "Good morning, Lawd!" in the (excellent) film of *Green Pastures.*

I've finished a book on Prayer.[1] Don't know if it is any good.

I'm glad you can still enjoy a new dress. I can still *dislike* a new suit.

In haste.

> Yours
> Jack

> The Kilns
> 19 May 63

Dear Mary

Sorry to hear of all your expenses. I have directed Harcourt Brace to send you a little extra. No time to write; my brother is ill and of course the mails have chosen that moment to be unusually heavy.

> Yours
> Jack

> Magdalene College,
> Cambridge
> 10 June 63

Dear Mary

I am sorry to hear of the acute pain and the various other troubles. It makes me unsay all I have ever said against our English "Welfare State", which at least provides free medical treatment for all. God's purposes are terribly obscure. I am thinking both of your

[1] *Letters to Malcolm: Chiefly on Prayer.*

116

sufferings and of the removal of such a Pope[1] at such a moment. And the horrid conclusions which some bigots on both sides will probably draw from it. My brother is away in Ireland. . . . This throws a lot of extra work on me, besides condemning me to—what I hate—solitude. God help us all.

> Yours
> Jack

> Magdalene College,
> Cambridge
> 17 June 63

Dear Mary

This is terrible news. The doctor who refused to come would, I think, be liable to criminal prosecution in this country.

Pain is terrible, but surely you need not have fear as well? Can you not see death as the friend and deliverer? It means stripping off that body which is tormenting you: like taking off a hairshirt or getting out of a dungeon. What is there to be afraid of? You have long attempted (and none of us does more) a Christian life. Your sins are confessed and absolved. Has this world been so kind to you that you should leave it with regret? There are better things ahead than any we leave behind.

Remember, tho' we struggle against things because we are afraid of them, it is often the other way round—we get afraid *because* we struggle. Are you struggling, resisting? Don't you think Our Lord says to you "Peace, child, peace. Relax. Let go. Underneath are the everlasting arms. Let go, I will catch you. Do you trust me so little?"

[1] Pope John XXIII.

117

Of course this may not be the end. Then make it a good rehearsal.

> Yours (and like you a tired traveller,
> near the journey's end)
> Jack

Dear Mary

Tho' horrified at your sufferings, I am overjoyed at the blessed change in your attitude to death. This is a bigger stride forward than perhaps you yourself yet know. For you *were* rather badly wrong on that subject. Only a few months ago when I said that we old people hadn't much more to do than to make a good exit, you were almost angry with me for what you called such a "bitter" remark. Thank God, you now see it wasn't bitter; only plain common sense. Yes: I do wonder why the doctors inflict such torture to delay what cannot in any case be very long delayed. Or why God does! Unless there is still something for you to do, as far as weakness allows. I hope, now that you know you are forgiven, you will spend most of your remaining strength in *forgiving*. Lay all the old resentments down at the wounded feet of Christ. I have had dozens of blood transfusions in the last two years and know only too well the horrid—and *long*—moments during which they are poking about to find the vein. And then you think they've really got in at last and it turns out that they haven't. (Is there an allegory here? The approaches of Grace often hurt because the spiritual vein in us hides itself from the

118

celestial surgeon?). But oh, I do pity you for waking up and finding yourself still on the wrong side of the door![1] How awful it must have been for poor Lazarus who had actually died, got it all over, and then was brought back—to go through it all, I suppose, a few years later. I think he, not St. Stephen, ought really to be celebrated as the first martyr.

You say too much of the very little I have been able to do for you. Perhaps you will very soon be able to repay me a thousandfold. For if this *is* Good-bye, I am sure you will not forget me when you are in a better place. You'll put in a good word for me now and then, won't you? It will be fun when we at last meet.

Yours
Jack

The Kilns
Frid. 28 June 63

Dear Mary

It was anaemia that endangered my life the winter before last, but of course trifling compared with yours. I think the best way to cope with the mental debility and total inertia is to submit to it entirely. Don't *try* to concentrate. Pretend you are a dormouse or even a turnip. But of course I know the acceptance of inertia is much easier for men than for women. We are the lazy sex. Think of yourself just as a seed patiently waiting in the earth; waiting to come up a flower in the Gardener's good time, up into the *real* world, the real waking. I suppose that our whole present life, looked back on from there, will seem only a drowsy half-waking. We are here in the land of

---

[1] Lewis was himself to experience a little more than a month later the unhappy closing of death's bright door before he could reach it. See letters of July 27 and August 10.

dreams. But cockcrow is coming. It is nearer now than when I began this letter.

> Yours
> Jack

> The Kilns
> 6 July 63

Dear Mary

... Do you know, only a few weeks ago I realised suddenly that I at last *had* forgiven the cruel school-master who so darkened my childhood. I'd been try-ing to do it for years; and like you, each time I thought I'd done it, I found, after a week or so it all had to be attempted over again. But this time I feel sure it is the real thing. And (like learning to swim or to ride a bicycle) the moment it does happen it seems so easy and you wonder why on earth you didn't do it years ago. So the parable of the unjust judge comes true, and what has been vainly asked for years can suddenly be granted. I also get a quite new feeling about "If you forgive you will be forgiven". I don't believe it is, as it sounds, a bargain. The forgiv-ing and the being forgiven are really the very same thing. But one is safe as long as one keeps on trying.

How terribly long these days and hours are for you. Even I, who am in a bed of roses now compared with you, feel it a bit. I live in almost total solitude, never properly asleep by night (all loathsome dreams) and constantly falling asleep by day. I sometimes feel as if my mind were decaying. Yet, in another mood, how *short* our whole past life begins to seem!

It is a pouring wet summer here, and cold. I can hardly remember when we last saw the sun.

Well, we shall get out of it all sooner or later, for
  even the weariest river

Winds somewhere safe to sea.
Let us pray much for one another.
                                   Yours
                                   Jack

                                   The Kilns
                                   9 July 63
Dear Mary

I can well understand with what mixed feelings
you received what was obviously, in the ordinary
medical sense very "good" news. Aren't you a trifle
fierce about the Doctor? It can't be much fun attempt-
ing to explain the details to 100 bio-chemical patients
who have no knowledge of bio-chemistry and who,
one knows, won't really understand, however hard
one tries. I was always only too glad to let mine off
with the merest skeleton account of my own state—I
found it such a boring subject. Also, aren't your doctors (like ours) hideously overworked? I know my
specialist, when I was in hospital, had a working day
which had begun at 8.30 a.m. and was still going on
at 9.45 p.m. Doesn't leave much elbow room.

Our hearts, by the way, must be different. When
yours is worst you have to lie flat. When mine was
worst I had to *sit* up—night and day for months.

By the way, as you come out I may possibly go in.
Swollen ankles—the Red Light for me—have returned. I see the doctor about this to-morrow. My
fear is that he will forbid me to go to Ireland on
Monday as I had arranged, and put me back in
hospital.

Our friends might really get up a sweepstake as to
whose train really will go first! Blessings.
                                   Yours
                                   Jack

Dear Mary

I go into hospital this afternoon. Think any sudden
change in my state is very improbable. Last time, the
repeated blood-transfusions got me past the danger
point, tho' they took much longer to do it than the
doctors expected. This time they will either take even
longer, or else they will fail to do it at all. I'm so
sleepy and tired that I feel very little concerned. The
loss of all mental concentration is what I dislike most.
I fell asleep 3 times during your letter and found it
very hard to understand! Don't expect to hear much
from me. You might as well expect a Lecture on
Hegel from a drunk man.

Yours
Jack

27 July 1963
Oxford
As from the Acland
Nursing Home

Dear Mary

Jack asked me to tell you that letter writing is
physically impossible, his fingers jerk and twitch so.
His physical crisis has greatly disordered his intelli-
gence and he is vividly aware of living in a world of
hallucinations. I am afraid it seems very difficult to
communicate to one another the high comforts. One
strange and beautiful reason is that I myself suffer so
little by their withdrawal. I have no physical pain—

only extreme lethargy and some sense of absurdity.

God bless you.

Yours,
Jack[1]

10 August 1963,
The Kilns,
Kiln Lane,
Headington Quarry,
Oxford.

Dear Mrs. ———

I am Professor C. S. Lewis's secretary writing to tell you some of the facts of Professor Lewis's present state of health. He felt that you were entitled to this history. I trust that you will not mind it coming from my hand; but so it must.

Professor Lewis had a relapse the second week in July. On the 15th of July he entered the Acland Nursing Home. During the last hours of the night he had a heart attack from which it was not expected by his doctors that he would emerge. He lay in a coma for nearly 24 hours breathing only because of an oxygen mask. As the Professor was incapable of receiving the Sacrament his priest administered Extreme Unction (2:00 p.m., 16th July). Contrary to the expectations of the medical staff, Professor regained consciousness at 3:00 p.m. (16th July) and asked for his tea. His state was still critical even though he revived somewhat during the next two days. Then followed a "black period" of dreams, illusions, and some moments of tangled reason. I hope it is clear to you that he was incapable of the normal exertions of correspondence.

[1] This letter is in the handwriting of Walter Hooper, who explains that the two voices are owing to an interruption during the dictation of the letter and his posting it before the error was noticed.

During the third week in the Nursing Home, Professor Lewis regained, very slowly, his rational faculties and, even slower, his strength. Last Tuesday (6 August) he was allowed to come home, accompanied, of course, by a nurse. Even though he is enjoying more ease and comfort at the Kilns Professor Lewis is, by no means, capable of writing letters or receiving visitors. He has with regret, but love for his College, resigned his Chair and Fellowship at Cambridge.

Professor Lewis regrets that he is unable at this time (and probably for a long time) to answer your letters. He is much concerned for you and prays that you may have courage for whatever may be yours both in the present and future.

I am, with prayers and affection,

> Yours faithfully,
> Walter Hooper

> The Kilns etc
> 30 Aug 63

Dear Mary

Thanks for yours of the 27. I am quite comfortable but very easily tired. B.B.[1] is still away so I have all the mail to do. So you must expect my letters to be very few and very short. More a wave of the hand than a letter.

> Yours
> Jack

---

[1] Lewis sometimes used these initials when referring to his brother.

Magdalen College
Oxford

27 / xi / 53

Dear Mrs. — — — — — — — Thank you for your letter
of Nov. 28. We have a good many things in
common at the moment, for I also am dead tired
(cab-horse tired) and I also have sinusitis.
I don't think we exactly "call it catarrh" over
here. Intense catarrh is one symptom of sinusitis,
and so none of us had heard of it. Till quite lately
I suppose cases of it used to be wrongly diagnosed
as mere catarrh. I find myself that when it procures
me more catarrh it produces heart pain & there
never comes a time when I sleep; do you find that so great.
about (if one can do it) is not to care whether
you sleep: sleep is a jade who scorns her suitors
but woos her scorners. I feel exactly as you
do about the horrid commercial rackets they have
made out of Christmas. I send no cards & give
no presents except to children

It is fine to see you agreeing with what you

believe to be my views on prayer: well you may for they are not mine but Scriptural. "Our prayers are God talking to himself" is only Romans, VIII, 26-27. And "praying to the end" is of course our old acquaintance, the parable of the Unjust Judge.

I am sure you will be glad to hear that your recent adventures have been a great support and "corroboration" to me. I am also v. conscious (as was especially so while praying for you during your workless time) that anxiety is not only a pain which we must ask God to assuage but also a weakness we must ask Him to pardon —or—for His bid us take no care for the morrow. The news that you had been almost miraculously guarded from that sin sd afford that from out hour a good hope that we shall all find the like mercy when our bad times come, has strengthened me much. God bless you,

yours

C. S. Lewis

Oct 9th 54

MAGDALEN COLLEGE,
OXFORD.

Dear Mary —————— Thanks for ye. letter of
the 6th., enclosing poem which I enjoyed. Fairies—
the people of the Shidhe (pronounced Shee)—are
still believed in in many parts of Ireland and
greatly feared. I stayed at a lonely bungalow
in Co. Louth where the road was said to be haunted
by a ghost and by fairies. That it was the latter
who kept the country people away, which gives you
the point of view— a ghost would be less alarming
than a fairy. A Donegal man told a parson I
know that one single when he was walking down
on the beach a woman came up out of the sea and
"her face was as pale as gold." I have seen a
leprechaun's shoe, given to a doctor by a grateful
patient. It was the length, and hardly more than the
breadth, of my forefinger, made of soft leather and
slightly worn on the sole. But get out of your
head any idea of comic or delightful creatures. They
are greatly dreaded, and called "the good people"
not because they are good but in order to propitiate
them. I have found no trace of anyone believing or even
having believed (in England or Ireland) in the tiny fairies

127

of Shakespeare, etc: are a purely literary invention, half-... are smaller than men, but most fairies are of human size, some larger. I don't forsee that a professorial chair or anything else will ever provide for a comfortable old age in this country. You see pensions and investments are taxed as "unearned income" and that leaves so little of them. It will be a pretty tough job translating a French book with no more knowledge of French than a dictionary can give! I don't see how any dict: will enable one to understand a phrase like <u>act ce qu'il y en avait</u>. Get the French tram... of whatever book you have in English (say the Bible) and try to get the hang of the language from that. Or perhaps the French bits... <u>Witch</u>, etc, etc. I couldn't... be more up to date & idiomatic. Between ourselves, I don't think you'll translate your French book very well, but you'll learn quite a lot of French in struggling with it and then your next attempt might be good. I wouldn't I'd... relieve any of your various troubles... but it is v. clear that the Holy Ghost is leading you through them all. With every blessing, yours

Jack Lewis